EXECUTIVE PRAISE FOR
NOT DOING LIST

"This is a really helpful book. Alex unlocks a new tool for professionals, managers, and executives to help them manage their most critical resource: time. *Not Doing List* gives you practical, effective ways to say no to the wrong things, so you can say yes to the right things."

—Mark McClain

Chief Executive Officer, SailPoint; best-selling author of *Joy and Success at Work: Building Organizations That Don't Suck (The Life Out of People)*

"Staying focused is hard in this fully digital, easily distracted work environment. *Not Doing List* outlines new and easy-to-implement tactics to help you stay focused and get ahead."

—Haniel Lynn

Chief Executive Officer, Kastle Systems

"Saying no to your boss is really hard. Alex outlines the fears that hold you back and gives you new tangible tips to make it routine, natural, and easy."

—Mary Abbajay

President & CEO, Careerstone Group LLC; author of *Managing Up: How to Succeed with Any Type of Boss*

"Brilliant minds understand the complex and explain it simply. Alexander is brilliant and so is his book. Saying no seems easy but is often hard. Once mastered, however, the power is awesome. His book, *Not Doing List*, is a must-read for anyone looking to supercharge their career or even just enjoy the things in life you love most."

—Bob Sicina
Professorial Lecturer, American University Kogod School of Business; former President of Latin America and the Caribbean, American Express

"We live in an always-on world—more data, decisions, stake-holders, and distractions. But we don't have more time. *Not Doing List* provides a tactical step-by-step guide to clearing out the unimportant so you can focus on key bets to help you pull ahead."

—René Gobonya
Chief Financial Officer, American Modern Insurance Group

NOT DOING LIST

NOT DOING LIST

Catapult Your Career by
Upping Your "No" Game

ALEXANDER BANT

Published by Advantage, Charleston, South Carolina.
Member of Advantage Media Group.

ADVANTAGE is a registered trademark, and the Advantage colophon is a trademark of Advantage Media Group, Inc.

Printed in the United States of America.

10 9 8 7 6 5 4 3 2 1

ISBN: 978-1-64225-244-6
LCCN: 2021900769

Book design by Wesley Strickland.

This publication is designed to provide accurate and authoritative information in regard to the subject matter covered. It is sold with the understanding that the publisher is not engaged in rendering legal, accounting, or other professional services. If legal advice or other expert assistance is required, the services of a competent professional person should be sought.

 Advantage Media Group is proud to be a part of the Tree Neutral® program. Tree Neutral offsets the number of trees consumed in the production and printing of this book by taking proactive steps such as planting trees in direct proportion to the number of trees used to print books. To learn more about Tree Neutral, please visit www.treeneutral.com.

Advantage Media Group is a publisher of business, self-improvement, and professional development books and online learning. We help entrepreneurs, business leaders, and professionals share their Stories, Passion, and Knowledge to help others Learn & Grow. Do you have a manuscript or book idea that you would like us to consider for publishing? Please visit **advantagefamily.com** or call **1.866.775.1696**.

To my mother, Marilyn Upah-Bant, the real author of our family,
who always had love and never enough time.

CONTENTS

ABOUT THE AUTHOR. xiii

INTRODUCTION: STRATEGY IS CHOOSING WHAT YOU WON'T DO 1

SECTION 1: REALLOCATE YOUR 168 HOURS

1: STOP TRYING TO "DO IT ALL". 13

2: DETERMINE THE OPPORTUNITY COST OF EACH HOUR 41

3: FIGHT THE FIVE FEARS THAT DRIVE US TO SAY YES. 51

4: SHIFT YOUR MINDSET FROM YES TO NO 61

SECTION II: BUILD YOUR NOT DOING LIST (NDL)

5: START WITH WHAT YOU WANT TO ACHIEVE 67

6: WRITE WEEKLY HEADLINES TO DEFINE THE
IMPORTANT THINGS YOU WILL DO 77

7: SELECT PROJECTS, MEETINGS, AND FLIGHTS FOR YOUR NDL. . . . 83

8: NAME COLLEAGUES, CUSTOMERS,
AND UNDERPERFORMERS FOR YOUR NDL 101

9: ADD INFORMATION, PROCESSES, IDEAS,
AND ROUTINE TASKS TO YOUR NDL 125

10: DESIGN A DISTRACTION-LESS WEEK 143

11: DECIDE WHAT CAN NEVER GO ON YOUR NDL. 159

SECTION III: STICK TO YOUR NOT DOING LIST

12: MAKE NOT DOING A HABIT BY CELEBRATING YOUR WINS 181

13: SAY NO WHILE BUILDING TRUST AND LIFTING OTHERS UP 189

14: BUILD HIGH-PERFORMING TEAMS WITH NDLs 215

CONCLUSION 243

APPENDIX: EXERCISES TO HELP YOU JUMP-START YOUR NDL 247

ABOUT THE AUTHOR

Alex is the Chief of Research for CFOs at Gartner (NYSE: IT), where his business insights are used by 45,000 leaders at a majority of the Global 500. His research teams quantify and share what the top companies and their leaders do differently to maximize their people, processes, and technology.

Alex has interviewed more than 3,300 C-level executives and led strategy sessions with more than 250 companies including: J&J, Boeing, Salesforce, Starbucks, GM, Disney, Heineken, Deere, Gilead, BMW, United Airlines, UPS, Philips, American Express, Verizon, Fidelity, McDonald's, Allstate, and L'Oreal. Alex's data and findings have been featured in Forbes, Wall Street Journal, The New York Times, Bloomberg, Fortune, Reuters, Business Insider, The Economist, Business Week, CNBC, Yahoo Finance, USA Today, and more than seventy-five other media outlets.

Alex holds a degree from the London School of Economics (LSE) and is an Adjunct Professor at American University's Kogod School of Business in Washington, DC.

STRATEGY IS CHOOSING WHAT YOU WON'T DO

Everyone gets 168 hours each week. You and Jeff Bezos. You and Beyoncé. You and Indra Nooyi. We all fight hard to spend these hours in a way that will help us get ahead. So how do some leaders accomplish so much more? They are simply better at saying no. They appear to do it all, when in reality they are laser focused on what they won't do. Their yes-to-no ratio is radically different from yours. This book helps professionals make the leap from leading with *yes* to leading with *no*. It's about starting each day with a deliberate list of things you won't do, as opposed to a list of things you need to accomplish. It's about ditching your to-do list and feeling great only about what you didn't spend time on. The goal of this book is to flip your brain's internal reward centers to start celebrating every low-value thing you delete, skip, dodge, cut, avoid, and don't do. Every day. This creates the capacity you need to focus on the things that truly matter. It's the only way to succeed in this always-on, fully digital, and easily distracted work environment. Reclaim your 168 hours. Catapult your career. Earn more. Live anxiety-free. All by upping your no game.

Trust me, I know. The struggle is real. The daily battle to try to do it all. We wage war against the clock hour by hour. I witness the struggle firsthand every day while helping C-level executives at more than 5,500 of the world's largest companies. Most days go something like this: you're shutting your laptop at 7:00 p.m. The sun is setting as you send one last email. You realize you still feel so behind. You feel like your day was wasted away with clearing out your inbox and sitting in at least four pointless meetings. You spent too long scrolling on your phone. You IM'd back and forth with a coworker for too long. A pointless news article consumed twenty minutes of your time. You agreed to help another team with an upcoming project, but you're not sure why. You and your boss sent the same deck back and forth six times, and it still feels incomplete. And your to-do list still has nine things left on it from yesterday. Damn. On top of all of this, you were supposed to run to Target and pick up birthday decorations, let the kids' school know about upcoming appointments, and schedule your car for an oil change. It's only Tuesday, and you still have three more days of feeling like this until the weekend. But, oh, wait. It's also performance review time. You were supposed to put feedback comments into Workday. You wonder how you'll find time to do that tonight or by multitasking during more meetings tomorrow.

This overloaded, distracted, hazy, "when does my to-do list end?" feeling carries over with you to the next morning. You roll over at 6:00 a.m. and slam your alarm. You grab some coffee and start to make a mental list of what you need to get done today. It's 8:00 a.m. now, and you look at your list. You think, *Okay, I got this. Today is the day. I'll make it through all this stuff, plenty of time!* You start checking your inbox. You get distracted reading a lengthy email. Your first meeting starts, and you burn the whole hour with no progress. You add three more things to your to-do list. Now your inbox is building up with people demanding a response. You sit through two more meetings. Three coworkers are IM'ing you across the morning for things they "really need." Twitter notifications are popping up left and right, and you can't stay focused. You work on a presentation for two hours after lunch, but you're not even sure the slides will be used. Before you know it, the sun is setting, and you have crossed only two things off your list. There you are again at the end of another day. You feel run over by the flood of requests, to-dos, meetings, and things that kept popping up. You close your laptop again. You feel like your time was robbed. In the back of your mind, you know you didn't make much progress toward your goals. And shit, you still didn't start those performance reviews.

Oh, you feel like this often? It's all good. Ninety-five percent of professionals feel this anxiety, and 74 percent report leaving the office without having the important things done.[1] And as the years go by, it gets harder and harder not to feel like this. There are exponentially more distractions, devices dinging, data to analyze, technologies to learn, processes to follow, and greater complexity required to get anything done. We feel like we are battling with ourselves and our to-do lists, fighting to get ahead. However, it's a choice to feel like this. This book is about choosing not to feel like this ever again. It's about stopping the madness.

We. Just. Throw. Away. So. Much. Time. In fact, McKinsey showed that most professionals spend 61 percent of their day emailing,

---

1   Alice Boyes, "5 Mental Mistakes That Kill Your Productivity," Harvard Business Review, November 4, 2019, https://hbr.org/2019/11/5-mental-mistakes-that-kill-your-productivity?utm_campaign=hbr&utm_medium=social&utm_source=facebook&fbclid=IwAR3qZ8KN4l1n-jvMh7ORuvHdYsSG6qcHKglFjJc9aOj7tuQ1s_bH3c4BgCA.

synthesizing information, and communicating with others.[2] We try to prioritize the important things, yet always feel behind and out of time. We sort. We organize. We calendar. We block time. Yet nothing seems to help us get ahead and feel in control. The truth is, we are tethered to our smartphones and laptops and lose focus repeatedly. We are addicted to checking our devices constantly. Our virtual door is always open, inviting anyone to steal five minutes or five hours. In just a few clicks, anyone can reach you anywhere, about anything. Our professional cultures remain "nice and polite," and we blindly default to saying yes to everything that comes our way. According to Adam Grant, a leading organizational psychologist at the Wharton School of the University of Pennsylvania, on average we

MOST PROFESSIONALS SAY YES MORE THAN 250 TIMES EACH DAY. BUT EVERY YES HAS A COST.

check email seventy-four time each day and switch tasks every ten minutes.

Can you join our working group? Yes. Can you make it to the meeting? Yes. Should we schedule a follow-up? Yes. Can we look at more data? Yes. Can you come make a presentation? Yes. Should we upgrade our current system? Yes. Should we launch the new product? Yes. Should we build a process around that? Yes. Can you respond to my email? Yes. Can we prep for the client call next week? Yes. Did you see my IM? Yes. Should I check my phone notifications? Yes. Should I hop on LinkedIn? Yes. Should I see what's trending on Twitter? Yes.

---

2   Michael Chui et al., "The social economy: Unlocking value and productivity through social technologies," McKinsey Global Institute, July 1, 2012, https://www.mckinsey.com/industries/technology-media-and-telecommunications/our-insights/the-social-economy.

Do you have a few minutes to chat? Yes. We burn through day after day with yes after yes, trying to shorten our to-do list at the same time.

In fact, most professionals say yes more than 250 times each day. But every *yes* has a cost. Your time. And you never get more time. Saying no became even harder when 84 percent of companies moved professional staff to remote working as a result of COVID-19. While working remotely, we become distracted more easily. When people can't see us being "busy" in the office, we default to saying yes to more distractions and low-value work in order to appear productive.

We say yes left and right and, at the same time, constantly search for answers to these questions:

- How do I end each day feeling accomplished?

- How do I stop procrastinating the important stuff?

- How do I avoid leaving work still stressed out?

- How do I feel in charge of my time, energy, and calendar?

- How do I get promoted?

- How do I take my career to the next level?

- How do I get back more time for family and things I love?

There are still too many business leaders, authors, and productivity gurus out there telling you what else you should do to advance your career and design a happy sustainable life. There are endless articles and books that proclaim things like, "The top three ways to work smarter," "Ten things unstoppable people do that others don't," "Sixteen lessons you never learned in school," "Five must-dos to get promoted," and "Seven habits for success." They offer endless motivational quotes and new techniques to get ahead. They all have a common theme: more, more, more. They tell you what everyone else is doing above and beyond what you are. They provide hacks to help you "do it all."

THIS BOOK IS FOCUSED ON ONLY WHAT YOU SHOULD NOT DO AND HOW TO NOT DO IT.

The approach in this book is quite the opposite. I want to help leaders do less. This book is focused on only what you should NOT do and how to not do it. Plain and simple. This is not another way to sort your to-do list. And it is not going to help you prioritize what work is important versus urgent. It's only about starting each day with a list of what you're NOT going to do. It will help you figure out what you can stop spending time on right now. What you can deliberately ignore. It will guide you to developing a mindset that will help you win back a large volume of precious hours by skipping, dodging, deleting, and avoiding the right things.

It's as simple as saying no. A lot. Sounds a bit odd, I know. But on face value it's also quite intuitive. Every no is actually allowing us to say yes to something more important that will grow our business and career. You know deep down that there are only a few important things you need to do to get ahead. Yet you struggle to stay focused on them. If you can define what you won't do up front, it will help ensure you spend time on the hard things that really need your attention. This book teaches you how to do that consistently. This book is about proactively deciding when and how to say no.

This might sound easy on the surface, but most professionals struggle to say no because it's high risk. Saying no to the wrong things can tank your performance. Saying no in the wrong way can destroy your reputation. It can burn relationships and maybe even end your career. Fear, guilt, and shame set in every time we're about to say no.

We think, *What if I say no to the wrong thing? What if I miss something important? What if the person doesn't like me as much after I say no? I won't look busy and they'll fire me. What if saying no hurts my chances of getting promoted? Will my boss really let me say no?* In reality, the much larger risk we face is saying yes too frequently to the wrong things and running out of time for what matters. Saying no and overcoming these fears requires a fundamental shift in our approach.

The only safe way to make this shift is with a Not Doing List or "NDL." This book is an end-to-end guide for building your NDL and using it consistently. The book provides frameworks, lessons, and approaches for starting each day, week, month, quarter, and year with a relentless focus on where you will not spend time and energy.

IN REALITY, THE MUCH LARGER RISK WE FACE IS SAYING YES TOO FREQUENTLY TO THE WRONG THINGS AND RUNNING OUT OF TIME FOR WHAT MATTERS.

Your to-do list, or "yes list," has helped you get this far in your career. To keep advancing, feel in control, and improve your happiness simultaneously, you need an NDL. To control your finances, you use a budget. To control your weight, you use a diet. To control your time, you use an NDL. It will empower you to say no left and right with confidence. Using an NDL will keep you focused on a small set of highly important things. It will help you win back vast amounts of time and rapidly excel in your career. This book will teach you the tips and tricks necessary to do a lot less while appearing like you're "doing it all."

It's not only about managing your time. Your NDL helps you focus your attention as well. It's your way of declaring proactively which things you won't pay any attention to. You have limited bandwidth to allocate each day, and your NDL defines where you won't waste any of it. Part of building your NDL requires naming the distractions that you will not let interrupt your focus, thus keeping your attention glued on the things that matter.

Harvard Business School professor Michael Porter wrote in his 1996 article "What Is Strategy?" that "The essence of strategy is choosing what not to do."[3] Your NDL is your strategy. It is the tool that allows you to focus your time and energy on the few things that matter. It is the key to pulling ahead in this overloaded work environment.

> THE ESSENCE OF STRATEGY IS CHOOSING WHAT NOT TO DO

In fact, a relentless focus on "not doing" is what has allowed many successful business leaders to build, grow, and scale the world's greatest companies. Steve Jobs is known for using a Not Doing List. During Apple's 1997 Worldwide Developers Conference (WWDC), Jobs shared that "Focusing is about saying 'no.' You've got to say 'no, no, no,' and when you say 'no,' you piss off people." His head designer, Jonathan Ive, shared how Jobs would often stop him in the corridors of the Apple Headquarters and ask him how many requests he had said no to on that particular day.[4] To Jobs, focus is not about force or willpower. It is about the ability to abandon a thousand great ideas to channel efforts into the one best idea at a time. An NDL helped Jobs make it through nearly eight hundred emails a day.

You might be thinking, *Okay, so I just make a list of what I won't do each week and try to stick to it?* Kind of. It's not that simple. Making

---

3   Michael E. Porter, "What is Strategy?" Harvard Business Review, November-December 1996, https://hbr.org/1996/11/what-is-strategy.

4   Zameena Mejia, "Steve Jobs: Here's what most people get wrong about focus," Yahoo Finance, October 2, 2018, https://finance.yahoo.com/news/steve-jobs-apos-most-people-124500367.html.

sure you don't pick the wrong things for your list is hard. Selecting enough of the right things is also hard. Diplomatically communicating what you won't do is even harder. Holding yourself accountable to not do the things on your list is really tough. Fighting off distractions left and right every hour requires true grit.

FOCUSING IS ABOUT SAYING 'NO.'

WHAT WE COVER IN THE BOOK

It's important to know up front that this book covers a strictly professional setting. It's not about marriage, dating, playing sports, raising kids, or your hobbies, interests, or personal life. You'll likely think of applications of this approach outside a professional setting, but we won't cover any explicitly.

First, the book will cover what an NDL is and what it is not and show you examples. Then it will dig into the five main fears that hold most people back from creating and deploying an NDL. The book then guides you step by step on how to create your own NDL and outlines common risks and traps to avoid. After that, we teach you how to hold yourself accountable for actually not doing the things on your list. The subsequent sections will teach you techniques for how to communicate what you're not going to do. And yes, we cover how to tell your boss no in a way that gains you credibility. Finally, it will show you how to teach your team and colleagues about an NDL and help them adopt this approach.

Let me be clear up front, this book won't prescribe to you what should be on your NDL. In fact, that's really difficult to figure out. The point of the book is to shift your mindset and give you a winning framework so you can identify things for your own NDL. I hope that after finishing this book your approach shifts from "What can I do to get ahead?" to "What can I skip, cut, avoid, and delete to make time for the few things that really matter to get ahead?" You may also be tempted to jump ahead and start making your NDL. You'll be a lot more successful with the concept by first learning about the value of your time, the fears that hold us back, and how to determine your yeses.

I'll make you a deal as we get started. If you invest roughly ten hours with this book and learn how to create and apply an NDL, it will generate at least twenty hours of things you can avoid doing in the next three months. That's a 100 percent return on your time in just twelve weeks. Carry this approach forward across the year, and you will have created two weeks of time back in your life. That's at a bare minimum. Grab a notebook or open a virtual note. As we go, we need somewhere we can put down all the low-value things that come to mind for your NDL.

You can also access NDL templates and additional productivity tools at notdoinglist.com.

Let's get started winning back your 168 hours!

SECTION 1

REALLOCATE YOUR 168 HOURS

CHAPTER 1

STOP TRYING TO "DO IT ALL"

You get paid in direct proportion to the difficulty of the problems you solve.

—ELON MUSK

YOU DON'T NEED TO "DO IT ALL" TO GET AHEAD

Most leaders have been brainwashed to believe that to get ahead and significantly increase their pay, they need to keep adding to their plate. Many leaders run around trying to get their name on more projects with larger scopes and more people to show more value. That's not how the best leaders get ahead. The best leaders know it's not about showing you can "do it all," but instead showing you can do the important things extremely well. Doing the few hard things that no one else will or can do (really well) will accelerate your career and pay rapidly. This is more difficult than ever in an always-on, fully digital, highly complex work environment. Doing one hard thing well, as opposed to doing an okay job on five things, is what will set you apart. Keep in mind that promotion and hiring decisions are not often comprehensive. The conversations that surround leadership performance are often based on only a few large factors and elements that stand out, not a laundry list of everything someone has done. Promotion and hiring conversations surround outcomes and impact on a few hard things that others gunning for the role did not do. Working longer hours or measuring the sheer volume of things you have completed leads to burnout, not advancement.

> DOING ONE HARD THING WELL, AS OPPOSED TO DOING AN OKAY JOB ON FIVE THINGS, IS WHAT WILL SET YOU APART.

NOT DOING AVOIDS BURNOUT

An NDL helps you advance more quickly, while also avoiding burnout. In 2020, the World Health Organization upgraded burnout from a "state" of exhaustion to "a syndrome" resulting from "chronic workplace stress" in its International Disease Classification. Employers seem alarmed by the phenomenon. A 2017 survey by Kronos found that 95 percent of human resource executives think that burnout is hurting efforts to retain workers.[5] An NDL is a key tool to feel less overwhelmed at work and improve our professional mental health.

In the book *Dare to Lead*, Brené Brown outlines the characteristics of "daring leadership," in which empathy, connection, and courage help leaders succeed. She covers the importance of rest, play, and recovery and encourages all leaders to stop celebrating pure volume

---

5   Richard A. Friedman, "Is Burnout Real?" The New York Times, June 3, 2019, https://www.nytimes.com/2019/06/03/opinion/burnout-stress.html.

of hours worked. She says, "Do not celebrate people who work through the weekend, who brag that they are tethered to their computers over Christmas break. Ultimately, it's unsustainable behavior, and it has dangerous side effects, including burnout, depression, and anxiety."[6]

Lindsay Grenawalt, chief people officer at a cloud-based computer software company, shared her perspective in a 2019 CNN investigation into employee burnout. She outlined that, "When you hire brilliant people, they will give everything to your business. It's on the business to say, 'Hold on, we don't want you to burn out. We want you here for the long haul and to do your best work.' You can't do that if you are exhausted and angry."[7] Leaders can help avoid burnout by keeping their employees focused on work that truly matters. To "focus" employees must make trade-offs. Your NDL is the tool to make these trade-offs on a daily basis.[8]

> STOP CELEBRATING PURE VOLUME OF HOURS WORKED.

An NDL will help you free up time to relax, recharge, and bring your A game to your job during the hours you work each week. We will explore how using the NDL is a key tool to help focus your working hours on the things that matter. This will allow you to take some of your free hours, and use them to refuel each week.

Let's take a quick look at how an NDL works in action.

---

6   Brené Brown, *Dare to Lead: Brave Work. Tough Conversations. Whole Hearts* (New York: Random House, 2018).

7   Kathryn Vasel, "More companies try four-day work weeks," Crossroads Today, July 2, 2019, https://www.crossroadstoday.com/more-companies-try-four-day-work-weeks/.

8   Kathryn Vasel, "Four day work weeks sound too good to be true. These companies make it work," CNN Business, July 1, 2019, https://www.cnn.com/2019/07/01/success/four-day-work-week/index.html.

WHAT EXACTLY IS A NOT DOING LIST?

Have you ever sat down and created a long to-do list? Most people have. In fact, it's how most people start their workday. You're probably great at creating the list. You flip to a new page in your notepad or on your phone and just brain-dump twenty-five things. It's not hard. In fact, if you're like most people, it calms your anxiety. You get all the things you are supposed to do out and down in a list. You probably find joy in putting your to-dos in categories and ordering them. Then you start plowing through the list. You smile a bit as you cross each thing off.

Your NDL is similar, but instead, it's a list of everything you won't do and won't let distract you. You sit down and create a long list of all the things you're not going to do or spend any time on. People you're going to dodge. Things you're going to skip. Distractions you're going to avoid. And notifications you're going to ignore. Sitting down to create your NDL starts with a simple question: What upcoming things can I not do? Safely, quickly, and with confidence.

Your NDL is a physical or electronic list of things you write down and commit to not doing. Like a to-do list, you cross items off when you skip or avoid them. You cross off the tasks that you decided you shouldn't do after you avoid doing them. Cross off meetings that you skipped. Cross off events you bailed on. Cross off the worthless networking you avoided. Cross off the name of the person you dodged who wastes your energy. The more things you can cross off that you didn't do the better. You will learn to feel accomplished based on the number of things you avoid wasting time on.

Later in the book, we will cover the following categories of things you should consider for your NDL:

- Meetings to decline

- "Energy vampires" to dodge

- Project teams to quit

- Presentations to skip

- Data to delete

- Work to send back to the correct owner

- Battles you should lose

- Customers you should proactively fire

- Networking events to avoid

- Business performance indicators to ignore

- Colleagues you'll delay a response to

- Time periods to put your phone down

- Emails to delete

- Anxiety triggers to spot and avoid

- Reports to stop producing

- Processes to simplify or automate

- Distractions to sidestep

- Work that should have a time limit set for completion

- Travel to cancel

- Business "problems" you'll ignore

- Proposals not to submit

- Personal performance gaps to not close

If you're thinking, What? This sounds like a bad idea, or Who would think like this? or even Wow, what kind of professional would do this? then please hang with me. I bet you have a lot of time that you need to start winning back. My aim is that by the end of the book you're asking yourself, why did I ever think it was okay to waste my time on these things before?

We'll help you carefully build your own NDL and show you how to effectively navigate your way through not doing everything on your list.

At this point an example NDL will help bring the concept to life. Here's an NDL for a work week in April from Cynthia, who's an advertising manager in Atlanta.

NOT DOING LIST—WEEK OF 4/13

MEETINGS/CALLS TO SKIP

- *Marketing roundtable Monday 10 a.m.*

- *New Division Townhall Tuesday 3 p.m.*

- *Plastics Inc. client call Tuesday 4 p.m.*

- *Meeting with Mary Wednesday 2:30 p.m.*

- *Rod Inc. client call Thursday 11:30 a.m.*

- *Fred catch-up Friday 2 p.m.*

- *Friday sharing session with LNA team Friday 3 p.m.*

THINGS TO NOT DO

- *Send in bullets for quarterly win list*

- *Fill out monthly web dashboard*

- *Skip the first hour of three-hour brainstorming session with PBB group Wednesday 3 p.m.*

- *Communications Round Up*

- *Don't create and send key recs dashboard*

- *Don't spend more than one hour on key customer segment map*

- *Don't run account reconciliation process manually; start to find a tech provider*

DISTRACTIONS TO AVOID

- *No email from 9 a.m. to 11 a.m. each day*

- *No IM from 2 p.m. to 5:30 p.m.*

- *Put phone on airplane mode 8 a.m. to 11 a.m. each day*

- *No Twitter until 3 p.m. each day*

THINGS TO IGNORE

- *Data from Tom about Q2 client retention in Asia*
- *Report from PwC partner*
- *Root causing any data related to UX in three-month rolling outlook*

EVENTS TO SKIP

- *Networking drinks Wednesday 6 p.m.*
- *Library association reception Thursday 6 p.m.*

PEOPLE TO AVOID

- *Nick Shapiro*
- *Sally Walker*
- *Bob Pana*
- *Deb Rowland*

By my tally, if Cynthia can avoid doing all these things this week, she's going to win back almost seventeen hours' worth of time. Impressive. Clearly, she's been applying this mentality for a while. She is bold enough to skip, dodge, not do, and avoid all these items and people this week. Can you imagine having seventeen hours back in your own week to spend on things that will help you get ahead?

Trust me, building this list is incredibly difficult and sticking to it is a constant battle. This book is your guide to getting started.

WE ARE NOT NEGOTIATING, PRIORITIZING, SORTING, OR DELAYING

Let's be clear, your NDL is not simply a list of what you don't *want* to do. You might even end up with items on your NDL that you're good at or enjoy. In fact, I'm sure that will happen quite frequently. Many leaders spend time on things they are comfortable doing and run to those activities out of instinct. An NDL is not a way to avoid the hard things. It's about breaking the rhythm of spending time on the easy things or things that waste your time. Hard things are considered hard because no one else usually wants to do them. This book is an important tool to help make sure you have time to run toward the hard things and advance your career.

An NDL is also not a list of things you wouldn't do anyway. It's not the things down at the end of your to-do list that you likely won't ever get to. Everyone has that random movie to see, book to read, club meeting to go to, or training to attend that they probably will never make it to anyway. Those don't go on your NDL. Your NDL is a list of things that you would have spent time on, done, or gone to. You are actively committing to not doing those things. Ever.

An NDL is not a way to negotiate less involvement in something. The items on your NDL are things you're committing to not do. Period. Don't fall into the trap of negotiating with yourself or others. You might be tempted to say, "Well, I'll go to the meeting and just multitask" or "I'll run the analysis, but for only one customer" or "I'll keep my IM open, but turn my dot red so people will hopefully avoid me" or "I'll send a canned response instead of nothing so they leave me alone." These are all traps. They trick us into multitasking, burning precious time, and letting people down halfway. An NDL is about placing bets. Daring to say no and move on. Our NDL helps us be purposefully binary in what we will and won't do.

An NDL is also not a way to prioritize what you will do. When a task, meeting, project, or event goes on the NDL, you actively avoid it. You never do it. Even if your time frees up, you still don't do it. You have named it and declared that you will absolutely under no circumstance spend time on it. Even when your work is finished at 2:00 p.m. one day, don't go back to the NDL and start spending time on things you committed to not do. Work on something harder.

If you're someone who procrastinates and you beat yourself up about it, then an NDL is vital to break the cycle. Your NDL is your list of low-value things and pending distractions that you now commit to not do. It won't let you fill your day with small meaningless tasks to procrastinate on your large goals. This forces our time and energy toward the hard, important things that matter for personal and professional growth.

Creating a solid NDL is a hard muscle to build. Everyone around you will continue to run around like a chicken attempting to do it all. This will make you anxious. You'll also likely pick the wrong things for your NDL from time to time. You'll likely still find yourself slaving to your to-do list certain weeks. This is not an absolute science. It's a different frame of mind and a strategy for how to spend your time differently. When applied, more often than not, it will get you ahead and give you countless hours back to spend on higher-value things.

If you're an executive or senior manager and have administrative support for scheduling, you might be thinking, Don't I pay someone to manage my calendar and be the gatekeeper of my time? Yes, but you as the leader still have to make hourly yes and no choices, coach your admin on how to build your NDL, and teach your team how to think like this.

YOUR NDL REPLACES YOUR TO-DO LIST

The hardest thing about using an NDL is breaking the cycle of feeling good after ~~crossing a plethora of small meaningless things off your list.~~ I won't lie; as I applied the NDL, there were nights of anxiety when I kept asking myself, *Did I do enough today?* There were early days when I'd feel like I didn't get a lot done. You'll have to retrain your mind to focus on outcomes and not measure the number of things crossed off your to-do list each day. Teach yourself to measure the impact on the right things and not give yourself credit for a list of small completed tasks or pointless meetings you went to. You'll see in the following NDL framework that a key facet is making sure you write down your NDL and go back and cross the items off when you successfully avoided them or didn't do them. A crossed out NDL should replace a to-do list crossed out with a lot of low-value things. Doing this will still give you a feeling of accomplishment and that "~~I crossed a lot of things off today~~" feeling.

So do you still need a to-do list once you have an NDL? To be honest, no. You can use one if you want for a while as you transition into using your NDL. This simply serves as a near-term crutch. If a list of the things to get done helps you "not forget anything" for now, then go ahead. However, my advice would be to make your NDL as a first step before you list what needs to get done. Then, a better technique is to put everything you still need to do on your calendar as an appointment with enough time to do it well. Then shred your to-do list and don't add to it. Only add time into your calendar when a new important task surfaces. Don't create a list. Use the time we freed up on our calendar to block time for the most important things we need to do. We will cover this later when we outline the steps for how to create your NDL.

HOW AN NDL WILL HELP YOU GET AHEAD, EARN MORE, AND FEEL IN CONTROL

You know that feeling? The happy, warm, low-anxiety, excited, positive-vibes feeling. The one you get when taking off on vacation, getting a raise, landing a promotion, ending a long project, closing a big deal, or completing an amazing workout. That first warm day of summer feeling. That feeling you get when seeing your kids play the lead role or hit the home run. The high points in life when you've worked hard and achieved success and can relax a bit. The NDL gets you that high feeling more consistently. It will yield that warm "Wow, I got a lot done today" feeling most days of the week. An NDL is about freeing up time so you can accomplish hard things and feel rewarded for doing so. You'll feel like you're making progress each day on things that matter to growing yourself and your career.

An NDL will also make your overall life a lot easier. Not every hour you win back has to be spent on more work. You can reinvest some of these hours in the things that bring you joy in the other parts of your life, as well. Less working on nights and weekends means more time with family. More vacations. More time on your hobbies. And you'll finally feel in control, no longer at the mercy of your mounting to-do list.

That's right, deciding what you won't do actually leads to more vacations, promotions, and happiness at the same time. That's why I'm perplexed by how some leaders operate without an NDL.

As you deploy your NDL week after week, you will naturally start thinking less about what you need to do and more about what you need to avoid doing. That's a great thing. It means you've flipped your mindset around to focus only on what matters.

FLIP YOUR COMPETITIVE PARANOIA

Former Intel CEO Andrew Grove famously liked to remind his employees, "Only the paranoid survive. Paranoia, when properly deployed, can serve as a powerful morale booster—even a competitive weapon—to organizations."[9] "Competitive paranoia," as the Mastercard CEO Ajay Banga calls it, propels our organizations to innovate and stay ahead of the competition. We all have competitive paranoia. And it's good for us. It's part of what drives us to get more done. In fact, we usually experience it at two altitudes. We want our company to beat the competition and on a personal level we want to pull ahead of peers for the next promotion, raise, or opportunity.

Here's the issue: we obsess about what others are doing to get ahead. We worry about what they are drafting, launching, building, winning, and achieving. We are paranoid about who are they meeting with, talking to, and forming connections with. We stew over what else are they joining, adding, buying, and promoting.

This often triggers us to think we're not doing enough. So we add, add, add, things to our plate. At a company level, we launch new initiatives. At a personal, level we just "grind" harder and try to pull ahead.

Have you ever worried about what the competition is NOT doing? You should.

You and the competition get the same 168 hours each week. They are not simply "working harder," they are likely working smarter. They're saying no to a lot of low

HAVE YOU EVER WORRIED ABOUT WHAT THE COMPETITION IS NOT DOING? YOU SHOULD.

9 Roderick M. Kramer, "When Paranoia Makes Sense," Harvard Business Review, July 2002, https://hbr.org/2002/07/when-paranoia-makes-sense.

value things. That is what has freed up their time to pull ahead. That is what should have you paranoid.

These are the questions that should be running through our head every day:

- What did the competition skip, dodge, delete or tune-out today that I wasted time on?

- How many hours did they win back this week? Did I win back that many too?

- What was their yes to no ratio this week and was it more balanced than mine?

WHO CAN AND CAN'T USE AN NDL?

YOU HAVE TO BE PERFORMING WELL

Do you typically meet your performance objectives at work? Do you constantly challenge yourself to get ahead? Do you find yourself wanting the next role or leadership position? If so, you're in a prime position to start using an NDL. But it's important to realize that this book is not for everyone. It's 301-level training for leaders or future leaders. I mention this because the NDL will get you into big trouble if applied under the wrong circumstances. If you're not a high-functioning professional who cares about your career and understands trade-offs and resource scarcity, this won't make much sense. If you don't have more valuable work to be doing professionally, this could illuminate the fact that your position is redundant. If you're struggling at work, you may not do the wrong things and hurt your performance even more. Also, putting the NDL into practice takes a high degree of emotional intelligence to navigate tense and complex situations.

Without self-awareness, you'll make enemies quickly. To use the NDL, you don't have to work a lot of hours, have a high-paying job, or be in a top management position. You just have to be performing well and have a desire to get ahead.

NDLs IN A HIGH-INTENSITY WORK ENVIRONMENT

In 2016, Erin Reid and Lakshmi Ramarajan studied high-intensity workplaces for a *Harvard Business Review* article.[10] They describe high-intensity workplaces as those where "managers routinely overload their subordinates, contact them outside of business hours, and make last-minute requests for additional work. To satisfy those demands, employees arrive early, stay late, pull all-nighters, work weekends, and remain tied to their electronic devices 24/7. And those who are unable—or unwilling—to respond typically get penalized."

They found that at these organizations 43 percent of employees simply accept the norm and truly eat, sleep, and live their work. Twenty-seven percent use the strategy of "passing," in which they work around the norm. They respond and give the impression that they are working (e.g., "Am on it—will take a few hours"). The rest, 30 percent, fall into the "reveal" category, where they openly share other parts of their lives outside the 24/7 grind. Seeking work-life balance, revealers ask for changes to schedules and workload. Performance reviews and promotion data showed that revealers, those who asked for less high-intensity, paid a substantial penalty.

An NDL is not about asking for a change in schedule or workload. It's not about asking to be less available for mission-critical work.

---

10 Erin Reid and Lakshmi Ramarajan, "Managing the High-Intensity Workplace," Harvard Business Review, June 2016, https://hbr.org/2016/06/managing-the-high-intensity-workplace.

It's not about choosing life over work. It's about focusing your work hours on the highest value things. That could be thirty working hours in a week or ninety. There might be times when you disagree with leaders about the best use of time in a "do everything" environment. Especially when you get the email at 2:00 a.m. You can still respond to email at 2:00 a.m. with an NDL. As long as you know up front that the email is tied to your focus areas and there are things you've said no to in order to gain time back. Don't disqualify yourself from using an NDL due to your company culture not really "allowing" it. Do you work at a start-up? A fast-growing tech company? A law firm? Maybe you're a teacher without enough resources. You need an NDL more than anyone.

An NDL works in high-intensity workplaces. In fact, it might even work better. The point of an NDL is to spend time on things that bring the most value to you and the organization. It helps eliminate low-value time drains. Senior leaders at high-intensity workplaces are usually laser focused on growing revenue and profit. That means avoiding low-value tasks has even more upside to your organization. If you've got the drive and motivation to work eighteen hours a day, at least get the best return possible for all the hours you're working. Now, we don't think you will have to actually work all eighteen of those hours if we do this right—we'll get there in a minute.

The key will be how you communicate the trade-offs you're making to leaders at a firm like this. We'll show you how to do that later. Once we get there, you may want to read that section twice if you work at a high-intensity firm.

SAYING NO IS IMPORTANT FOR ALL LEADERS, REGARDLESS OF BACKGROUND

Different cultures, generations, and genders have predisposed notions of when they should and should not say yes and no. Your heritage, upbringing, and cultural norms will make you more or less comfortable saying no to seemingly low-value things in a professional setting. The NDL framework is for all leaders, regardless of these traditions. Your background may mean you want to take more or less risk with your NDL. It will also mean your communication approaches may need to be tailored. At the end of the day, there is no one group that should feel not permissioned to apply the NDL in their professional life.

YOU HAVE TO BE WILLING NOT TO PROCRASTINATE

Your NDL is all about helping you focus on the hard things that will help you get ahead. By clearing out low-value tasks, you have to be willing to then spend the regained time on the hard things that align with your goals. You can't create an NDL, then turn around and burn the time you gained on low-value work or distractions. You also can't use your freed-up time procrastinating on the hard things you should go do. You have to replace the time you win back with things that tie back to your goals, objectives, and personal growth.

> **YOU HAVE TO REPLACE THE TIME YOU WIN BACK WITH THINGS THAT TIE BACK TO YOUR GOALS.**

NDLs ARE VITAL FOR THOSE BILLING THEIR CLIENTS HOURLY

I was explaining the concept of an NDL to a partner at a large law firm in New York. She said, "If I skip out on doing things, then I'm just billing clients less, which hurts our profits." Not so fast. If you're in a role where you bill clients directly for the hours you work, an NDL will help you grow your business. In three ways actually. First, you can bill more for higher-value, mission-critical work. To do that, you should be saying no to a lot of low-value repeatable things. This will free up time to help your client solve larger, complex higher-price-tag problems. Second, an NDL can and should be used to determine what nonbillable activities you can avoid. If applied to the nonbillable aspects of your workflow, it will free up time that you can then allocate toward billable hours. Finally, your NDL will help you proactively fire your least profitable customers altogether. We'll cover that one in detail coming up.

IF YOU'RE NEW TO AN ORGANIZATION OR TEAM, YOUR NDL IS VITAL

At the end of a 2021 presentation about NDLs, a newly hired data scientist made the following comment. They said, "I'm new; I have to just do everything I'm asked to do and go to all the meetings I'm invited to." I hate hearing this. It's not true. What is true is when you first join an organization, you define and set the tone for where and how you spend your time. Of course, you want to fit in, be liked, and learn as much as you can. But blindly doing everything that comes along will be much harder to unwind later. The tactics you learn in this book are vital to starting a new gig, because they help define how your time should and should not be used. Don't wait until you feel comfortable in your role; use an NDL starting on day one. It will elevate your career trajectory and ensure you can accomplish more during your tenure at the organization.

NDLs WORK FOR JUNIOR LEADERS TOO

Yes, it is easier to not do more things the more senior you are within an organization. You obviously have more autonomy over how you spend your time and which tasks and projects you work on. However, the sooner you can learn the NDL framework and apply it to your day-to-day, the faster you will be able to advance. If you're a less-tenured leader, your NDL may be only a few things each week. If you can find even just a few hours of things not to do each week, it will translate into hundreds of hours back each year. If you reinvest those hours back into the hard things and critical tasks for your own development, you will advance faster than others.

For newer leaders, an NDL is a great tool for understanding the return on your time, learning to focus on the things that matter, and saying no to unimportant meetings, people, initiatives, and projects. Building this muscle early in your career will give you a leg up as your role becomes more complex and demands on your time start to grow. Those around you will continue slogging their way to the next promotion (that likely won't happen), while trying to do everything. Their to-do list will expand until they drown or burn out. Meanwhile, you'll feel focused and relaxed while smiling at your next pay increase.

WHY AN NDL OUTPACES OTHER POPULAR TIME MANAGEMENT TECHNIQUES

The NDL leapfrogs many other popular time-management methods and can help you save abundantly more time. And arguably, it is much simpler and easier to implement. Let me contrast an NDL with a few of the most prominent works on personal effectiveness, focus, and time management so you can visualize the impact of using an NDL.

For example, *The 7 Habits of Highly Effective People*, first published in 1989, is a business self-help book written by Stephen Covey. Covey teaches readers to use a two-by-two matrix to organize all activities and tasks. It was adapted from the Eisenhower Matrix, created by Dwight D. Eisenhower, a five-star general during World War II and thirty-fourth president of the United States. The four-quadrant matrix helps you organize your tasks and determine which to prioritize based on urgency and importance of the task. Urgency and importance make up the axes of the two-by-two. You place all your to-dos in the four quadrants on the matrix. Tasks that fall into the not important and not urgent part of the matrix are what is considered "left over" or "things that come last." People take their long list of to-dos and reorder them with this matrix. Then they reorder them again, then again, then again.

The fundamental flaw when adopting this framework is that you still are permissioned to think, *How much can I do?* and *What order should I do all these things in?* Thinking this way is the opposite of being on the hunt for what you can cut, delete, skip, and avoid up front, before you even build a list. So instead of taking a list of to-dos and sorting, sorting, and sorting again, spend more time predetermining what you won't do in the first place. An NDL is about developing a method to proactively go hunting day by day and week by week for activities, meetings, events, and distractions that you will proactively not do. Using an NDL helps you set up a reward mechanism to give yourself credit and praise for not doing low-value things. And feeling great about it.

Many professionals also lean on the time management method Getting Things Done (abbreviated to GTD), which was created by David Allen. The GTD method helps you take work and break it into actionable tasks. Allen posits a complex decision tree that guides

USING AN NDL HELPS YOU SET UP A REWARD MECHANISM TO GIVE YOURSELF CREDIT AND PRAISE FOR NOT DOING THINGS.

you to place these tasks in the following buckets in this specific order: the someday/maybe list, a reference list, a list of tasks to do, a "delegate to someone else" list, an "on your calendar" list, and the "trash list." The method works, and millions of professionals apply it. However, did you notice how the trash list is considered last? GTD only helps you organize your list. It is a method for sorting and categorizing. It helps take the few small leftover things and place them in the trash. You're tempted to still try to "do it all" with this approach. On the contrary, an NDL starts with the trash and puts it first, before any sorting can begin. Using an NDL is about always hunting and screening everything to be placed in the trash first, not just what's left over. Using an NDL is not about ordering, sorting, categorizing, and color coding. It's about entering each week and waking up each morning hunting for things to not do or avoid.

Next, you may have heard the term *Eat the Frog*, inspired by a famous Mark Twain quote, "Eat a live frog first thing in the morning, and nothing worse will happen to you the rest of the day." In a famous book on avoiding procrastination, author Brian Tracy details why and how you should tackle your most challenging task in the morning. Again, Eat the Frog is a tool to help you shuffle your to-dos so they are in an order that makes the most sense. It helps you pick and start with the hardest tasks of the day. However, you're still left trying to do more, more, more across the day. With an NDL in place, you're eliminating low-value work before it would even end up on a list of things to be sorted. Instead of assuming you must eat the frog, with an NDL you might question, Can I just not eat the frog at all?

There is also a popular self-help book by Timothy Ferriss, *The 4-Hour Workweek: Escape 9–5, Live Anywhere, and Join the New Rich.* Ferriss includes over fifty practical tips and real-life case studies on how you can live more and work less. He refers to this approach as "lifestyle design." He disagrees with the traditional deferred life plan, in which people work grueling hours and take few vacations for decades and save money in order to relax during an early retirement. He helps you win back time, but all in the aim of having to work less. His book is about how to do the bare minimum from a remote location so you can live like a retiree earlier. To be clear, an NDL is not about trying to work less than forty hours a week. Instead, an NDL is about freeing up time and reinvesting those hours in the things that will grow your career. It's about feeling focused and accomplished because you worked on only the hard things required to advance and get ahead. It's not about skipping meetings only to then lie on the beach.

Using an NDL is also stronger than setting a boundary, and there has been extensive research, as well as many self-help books, about setting boundaries. Most of the books are written to help those with emotional trauma or social anxiety. Most research on boundary setting has a slant toward making sure you're cutting out the right people and substances from your life and ditching emotional baggage. In a *New York Times* Best Selling book, *Boundaries*, Drs. Cloud and Townsend unpack the ten laws of boundaries, showing you how to bring health and happiness into your relationships. They set out to answer questions like, Can I set limits and still be a loving person? What if someone is upset or hurt by my boundaries? And aren't boundaries selfish? These are all great questions but distant from simply saying no in a professional setting. An NDL is not a social boundary. This book covers purely the leadership side of winning back time. Being blunt and saying no. It does not cover the emotional complexity of fixing social tension in your personal life. As part of your NDL, it's important to dodge individuals in a work setting that drain your time and attention, but that's only one piece of a much larger puzzle. The NDL is a broader list of tasks, meetings, activities, events, and processes you will not spend any time on in a given week.

As I was personally learning to master my NDL, I read a powerful book by Laura Vanderkam titled *168 hours: You Have More Time Than You Think*. Her research looks at the truth of modern life and the fact that we are starved for time. She studied how successful people allocate the 168 hours they have each week. She looked at the nature of modern families, sixty-hour workweeks, and 24/7 connectivity. She observed that even as the world becomes more complex and we have less time, people say they'd like to read more, get to the gym regularly, try new hobbies, and accomplish all kinds of goals. But then they give up because there just aren't enough hours to do it all. They start to feel bad about it too. She wanted to figure out how some people are able to keep it all together and advance at the same time.

After interviewing dozens of successful, happy leaders, she realized that they allocate their time differently than most of us do. They understand the ROI of their time. They start by making sure there is time for the important stuff. They prioritize work and tasks at home based on what they do well. They align their 168 hours with their strengths and core competencies.

Vanderkam endeavors to help people sleep eight hours a night, exercise five days a week, take piano lessons, and write a novel, without giving up quality time for work, family, and other things that really matter. The key is to start with a blank slate and to fill up your 168 hours only with things that deserve your time. Vanderkam shares creative ways to rearrange your schedule to make room for the things that matter most. Her work focuses on shifting your calendar around and outsourcing certain tasks. You build a perfect calendar each week based on your strengths. I tried her approach for several months, and it felt more like playing Tetris with my calendar. I found myself still trying to fit in a lot of things across the week that really shouldn't have earned my time or attention at all.

I would argue that Vanderkam does not go far enough. Her framework focuses on allocating time across the week but does not account for the countless distractions that pop up every hour. This is where your NDL comes into play. It is important prework to determine what won't get allocated at all and which distractions you commit to avoid. Your NDL will help you spot all the things you can just delete up front. After you've decided what you're not going to do, the allocation of your time is a lot simpler because you've removed all the low-value items. You're finding slots on your calendar throughout the week only for the things that matter. Fewer things. More important things. Things worthy of your precious time. Vanderkam's philosophy aligns well with using an NDL. I just found that her approach focuses more on what you should spend time on, as opposed to what we flat out should not do.

In *Essentialism*, Greg McKeown shows you how to achieve what he calls the disciplined pursuit of less. It is a systematic way to determine what is absolutely essential and eliminate everything that is not. This allows you to make the highest possible contribution toward the things that really matter. Think of your NDL as the tool that allows you to pick out the non-essential and commit to not spending time on those things. Our books pair well together to help you focus on what really matters.

The 7 Habits of Highly Effective People, *Getting Things Done*, *Eat That Frog!*, *4-Hour Workweek*, *Boundaries*, and *168 Hours* all offer great methods for how to prioritize a mountain of to-dos and help you focus, screen tasks, and play to your strengths. However, many of the methods mentioned were helpful when we scheduled meetings on physical calendars, read paper newspapers, had a rolodex, made to-do lists on lined stationary, used landlines, and set reminders by sticking Post-it Notes all over our desk. The methods covered by the other authors also assume that your time is just allocated across a list of known and static tasks, when in reality most of your time is drained by last-minute meetings that didn't need to happen, endless notifications popping up, digital distractions, or people bothering you. Those things never make it on your matrix, into a list, or in the trash.

NDLS ARE REQUIRED IN A DIGITAL WORLD

Living in an always-on fully digital world means we need a new approach to fight back against the flood of inbound questions, requests, data, and distractions. We go through the day with notifications dinging, people IM'ing us, emails popping up on our smart watches, lists on our digital refrigerator screens, Alexa reading us the news, logging into cloud servers, and people messaging us on five different apps. Most of us already can't put down our smartphones. Email volume and bursts of digital distractions online can eat your whole day away. Just imagine how connected and plugged in we'll feel in the years to come. Living in this fully digital world means you need a bolder and more comprehensive approach to focus and get ahead. Winners will be defined by those who are able to avoid the right things and focus their time and attention on the things that matter for success. You can think of your NDL as your shield or defense mechanism in this world of expanding demands for

LIVING IN AN ALWAYS-ON FULLY DIGITAL WORLD MEANS WE NEED A NEW APPROACH TO FIGHT BACK AGAINST THE FLOOD OF INBOUND QUESTIONS, REQUESTS, DATA, AND DISTRACTIONS.

your time and attention. It means your NDL is the fastest path to getting the right things done in this always-on digital world. It will help you rapidly reduce the volume of tasks, meetings, and distractions in advance of sorting, categorizing, prioritizing, or color coding. An NDL also helps you proactively spot when your time and attention will be robbed and to design your day in a way that protects it.

Now, there are blogs and articles about how to say no and create a list of things you won't do. Don't get me wrong, this concept is not unheard of. However, most of the coverage is about a list of things to say no to in personal areas, such as dating, daily routines, working out, or saving money. These blogs and articles don't get into the dynamics of saying no in a professional setting and address the fears that hold us back. They also make it sound easy. They fail to recognize how truly hard it is to say no. Most of these works lack awareness about how hard it is to come up with the list, say no effectively, and hold yourself accountable. This is why I wrote this book. This book gets into the hard things about saying no, leaving you empowered to start doing it more confidently and consistently.

We'll get to creating your NDL shortly. Before that, we need to see how much your time is actually worth. Understanding the value of your time in a financial way will help you push harder to find more things to not do each day. Let's put a price tag on your time.

CHAPTER 2

DETERMINE THE OPPORTUNITY COST OF EACH HOUR

The art of leadership is saying no, not saying yes. It is very easy to say yes.

—TONY BLAIR, FORMER PRIME MINISTER
OF THE UNITED KINGDOM

Tempus is a word unique to Latin that denotes a dual meaning: "time," as well as "opportunity." Your 168 hours present an opportunity each week. An opportunity to control your time and allocate it as a resource. This section is about figuring out the cost of throwing that opportunity away.

I have a coffee mug that reads, "You have as many hours in the day as Beyoncé." I leave it face out on my desk. Everyone awkwardly stares at it when we're in meetings, and many colleagues have asked what it means. I always answer with, "Think about how many times Beyoncé must have to say no each day!" Sure, she has help from a large team, but she must allocate the same twenty-four hours in the day that you and I both have. The difference is she is ruthless with her time. She has to say no well over one hundred times for every time she says yes. The mug reminds people to stop and think about the time they are allocating to whatever we're discussing. It's a reminder that defining what you won't do is the most critical leadership task of all.

TREAT YOUR TIME LIKE YOUR FINANCES

"How you spend your time is more important than how you spend your money. Money mistakes can be corrected, but time is gone forever." This quote is from David Norris, an Irish scholar, independent senator, and civil rights activist. It's more specific than the old favorite, "time is money." The quote reminds us how ironic it is that many people treat their time as unlimited and money as scarce. In reality, it's quite the opposite.

I'm sure at one point or another you have created a budget. You may still use one regularly. When you make a budget, you take your income and then decide how much you're willing to spend in certain categories. You make trade-offs about what is more and less important. Then you see if you can stick to what you budgeted. Allocating a scare amount of money across competing priorities forces you think, *I've got to stop eating out so much* or *I have to stop buying as many suits* or *I need to cool it on the shoes* or *I need to cut back on the cocktails*, and so on.

It's quite simple if you think about it. A budget is essentially a Not Spending List (NSL). By putting a budget down on paper, you're essentially declaring that you're NOT going to spend as much money on certain things. In essence, we're allocating a scarce set of dollars toward things that matter. The things that matter less don't get our money. And inherent in this allocation you are setting is a limit about what you're willing to spend. You declare things like, "I won't eat out this weekend," or maybe you decide to watch Netflix instead of spending twelve dollars on a movie ticket. You bring leftover meals for lunch to avoid the eleven dollars you would spend at the salad bar. You don't buy the latest iPhone model because it seems lavish. You don't buy the sports car you want to keep your monthly bills down. You skip the five-star dining and eat at the local bar instead. You make these choices rationally because you'd rather have more money in your pocket each month. Every time you see a price, you either consciously or unconsciously are evaluating, *Do I have room in my budget? Is it worth it? Should I spend that much?*

TIME IS SCARCER AND THEREFORE MORE VALUABLE THAN MONEY.

So why don't people do the same thing with time? Every time someone sees a project, request, meeting, event, or potential distraction, why don't they question the cost in terms of their time? Remember, time is scarcer and therefore more valuable than money. You can always go into debt or earn more money. You can't do that with time. Everyone has a fixed amount, so allocating it should be even more important than budgeting money.

Having a clear set of things you won't spend money on means you inherently have the self-control to get these trade-offs right. Why do most people struggle to declare with confidence where they won't spend time like they do with their money? Time is hard to quantify, it's hard to measure the return, most people don't understand the value of their time, and many people don't think they have as much control as they really do. All fine answers for now, but our time (unlike money) has limits, and you can't ignore that.

Just as your mind is trained to not go out and spontaneously spend five hundred dollars on designer shoes, you have to train your mind to not let you burn two hours in a pointless meeting. That's where the NDL comes into play. You don't need to budget all your time like you might do with your monthly income. You just need to declare where you will no longer spend time. Coming up, we'll start creating your first NDL, which will show you sustainable ways to decide where you can stop spending your time. Spotting things to say no to will soon be as easy as knowing you can't blow your whole paycheck on a shopping spree.

To make this concept more powerful, let's see how much an hour of your time is worth. Having a value associated with units of your time will help you say no faster and more frequently.

YOU'RE THROWING AWAY AT LEAST $600,000 EACH YEAR

Have you ever thought about the financial return on your 168 hours in a week? Or better yet, what it could be? Have you actually done the math to figure out what each one of those hours is worth? It has to be a large sum. We learned earlier from the McKinsey report that nearly 61 percent of time is spent emailing (28 percent), synthesizing information (19 percent), and collaborating (14 percent). Really? Sixty-one percent of our week on these three tasks. What a waste. We need to put these hours to work in a more productive way.

Let's do some math together. Doing this will illuminate how much the misallocation of even just one hour might be costing you.

There are two approaches to estimating the cost of an hour of your time. The first is a direct-cost approach, and the second is an opportunity-cost approach ... yes, you're having flashbacks to the economics courses you took years ago. Hang tight.

From a direct-cost perspective, you're looking through the lens of the company or organization that you work for. You're assessing the direct cost to your employer for a misallocated hour. Essentially, what does a wasted hour cost your employer? If you're in a billable role, assume for this scenario that any billable hours are held constant and we're only looking at internal costs to your organization for hours spent on nonbillable work.

I'll use an example to show how it's calculated. Assume you earn $100,000, plus the organization pays another $30,000 for your benefits and overhead (other company expenses to employ you). So your total employee cost is $130,000. I know this might be high for some readers, but it will allow you to calculate the cost for your own salary more easily if we start with a round number. Assume you work 240 days in a year, with paid leave, holidays, and weekends. Then your daily cost to the organization is $542 ($130,000/240). If you work eight hours a day, then your time costs the company $68 an hour. You can manipulate these variables to figure out the cost of an hour of your time to your organization. That means every hour someone wastes in this scenario costs the organization at least $68. Multiply that by the number of attendees in a given meeting or on a project, and you'll see how this adds up. You'll see how several low-value meetings a week can cost the organization thousands of dollars. For example, five people working on a project for ten hours a week for a month has a direct cost of $13,600.

This might not sound like much. And in the grand scheme of things, this really isn't that costly for most organizations, depending on their size and funding. However, this is assuming you just burned that hour doing nothing. It was just lost forever with no other work being completed. It assumes you produced nothing of value to the company for that time. You and your colleagues are only throwing away a few thousand dollars a day on time-wasting activities. Fine. The leaders of your organization are probably burning more than that on their next business-class ticket or lavish client dinner. This lost time and cost is not going to make a large dent in profits. Frankly, most organizations are not scrutinizing costs at this level anyway. However, this doesn't capture the potential benefit of you spending that hour on something valuable.

Now, let's take a look at the other approach, measuring the opportunity cost. Opportunity cost, for those trying to remember your intro economics courses, is defined as "the loss of potential gain from other alternatives when one alternative is chosen." Time is scarce. For every hour you spend on one project, there's an alternate project you could be working on. For every meeting you sit in, there's an alternate meeting you could be sitting in. For every presentation you build, there's another you could be building. When calculating the value of your time, you want to measure the value of using your time in another way. We want to understand how much higher the return will be on your time if you allocate it to alternative activities, clients, meetings, and projects. Let me show you the economic value (or upside) you can create if you allocate that time to higher-return activities.

Here we'll measure the upside of spending your time on better alternative tasks and projects within the four walls of your company or organization. To do this, let's estimate the potential positive value you can create and then divide that by the hours allocated to that alternative project or initiative. Let's assume you found ten hours' worth of things to put on your NDL in a given month. Those ten hours were then redirected to higher-value work. That would equate to about thirty minutes per working day of time gained back and reallocated during that month. Honestly, finding thirty minutes per day will be easy once you're using an NDL consistently. Assume you then used those ten hours to help launch a new marketing campaign, win new business, secure a strategic partnership, or solve an internal process bottleneck. Maybe you renewed a contract, generated fifty new marketing leads, unlocked new data, found a way to automate a process, or created a new asset or product feature. The positive value could range quite a bit in terms of monetary return and value to your organization. No doubt that it's hard to estimate. But say you were able to earn or save the organization another $25,000 by spending those ten hours on this alternative initiative. That would mean you're now generating $2,500 ($25,000/10 hours) of upside an hour by spending time on the higher-value alternative.

Annually, that's $300,000 in potential positive value from shifting thirty minutes per day. Yes, only thirty minutes per day. That's easy with an NDL. If you can find sixty minutes (one hour) of low-value items to not do each day that would yield twice as much, or $600,000 in annual upside for your organization. What if a team of five did this? Now we're talking about over $3 million in value created by shifting one hour per day to higher-value work. That is only twenty hours a month, five hours a week, or one hour per day. That's incredible. One hour per day reallocated to the most important things for your organization yields substantial returns. A small team that creates a list of what they won't do will yield $3 million more in value than a team that is not focused. And that's without much effort.

No wonder the people who allocate their time well move into senior management positions faster. This $600,000 in value creates a 4.6x return on your total employee cost of $130,000. And this is just the beginning. Once you get your NDL up and running, finding one hour per day of things to put on your NDL will not be hard. You can manipulate these variables based on what you earn, what you can accomplish with your reallocated hours, and the amount of time you think you can win back. Come up with your number. It doesn't matter if a reallocated hour is worth $500 or $500,000. It also doesn't matter if it's precise. Whatever the number is, it will empower you.

I included this analysis to build excitement about the benefits of an NDL. Even if your NDL leads you to find only one hour per day of things to not do, you could see a 4.6x financial return to your organization. This should quickly translate into more opportunities and pay for you personally. This approach to hourly cost and value may not fit for everyone. You can also run the same simulations on value delivered to your clients, your organization's impact on the community, or donations brought in. There are countless ways to measure value, and it will be measured in a unique way by each organization. The point still holds. There is huge upside in using your NDL to find even one hour per day and reallocate that hour to higher-value work.

Keep this upside opportunity in mind next time someone requests your time. When you and four colleagues receive the next hour-long meeting invite, stop and think, *Is this meeting really worth at least $10,000 to our organization?* Having to justify that should help make no more automatic.

IS THIS MEETING REALLY WORTH AT LEAST $10,000 TO OUR ORGANIZATION?

PAY YOURSELF A TIME DIVIDEND

We saw how much your employer can benefit from your using an NDL. What about yourself? Shouldn't you get a reward too? Yes. The math assumes you reinvest all saved hours right back into other work. But the real win-win is to take a fraction of that time for yourself, as well. You can skip five hours of meetings, projects, and initiatives per week and use some of that time for you personally. The goal is not to work less than forty hours per week, but maybe you can leave the office earlier and see your kids. Maybe you can head out on your vacation a day early. Maybe you can meet a friend for coffee. Maybe you can finally take some time to reflect. Maybe you can do things that reinvest in you.

If you work for a smart organization, taking back a few of the hours that you free up from low-ROI activities won't be seen as a bad thing. We just learned how critical it is to avoid burnout. As long as you're running hard at your critical priorities, your organization is (hopefully) not making sure it takes you a certain number of hours to accomplish your goals. So why not use a bit of that time for yourself? Invest in a few things that bring you joy and fulfillment.

Your organization will be benefiting immensely, you'll feel in control at work, you'll be working on things that get you ahead professionally, and you'll be paying yourself a dividend of some of the freed-up time. That is a recipe for sustained low anxiety.

Hopefully, putting some math behind this has lit a fire inside you. There is huge financial upside coupled with lower anxiety when we use an NDL. It should be clear that you need to start winning back your time and reinvesting it. You may even think you're ready to put down the book and draft your NDL for tomorrow. Not yet. Let's jump to the fears that hold most people back from doing this easily. Being able to recognize the natural instincts that make it hard to say no will help us overcome them. Then we'll get you up and running with your first NDL.

CHAPTER 3

FIGHT THE FIVE FEARS THAT DRIVE US TO SAY YES

Freedom comes when you learn to let go, creation comes when you learn to say no.

—MADONNA, SINGER, SONGWRITER, AND ACTRESS

If your NDL can help you gain back so much time, why doesn't everyone do it naturally? Because saying no is really hard for most people. You like to think you can wake up one morning and just start saying no with ease and avoid things left and right. It doesn't happen like that for most people. There are inherent forces that hold us back each day from simply saying no more often.

At the root of our inability to say no is fear. Fear of missing out, fear of confrontation, fear of not looking busy, fear of change, and fear of failure. When I talk to professionals about why they don't use an NDL, they tell me that these five fundamental fears hold them back from running toward saying no more frequently. These fears act as mental roadblocks to getting started. When you go to say no or not do something, these fears kick in and propel you back to saying yes. Let's review these one by one and then apply techniques to overcome them.

FEAR 1: FEAR OF MISSING OUT (FOMO)

Skipping something that could end up being important

One of the first fears that will strike when you go to make your first NDL is the fear that you'll skip, delete, or dodge something that ends up being important later. You'll think, *Maybe it's better to go to the meeting, join the project team, attend the reception, meet with the client, or complete the dashboard because I or someone else might miss something.* This fear is overcome only by trying to gain as much intel about the thing you're going to say no to, followed by trial and error. To overcome this fear, ask as many questions in advance as you can about agendas, attendees, focus, impact, and scope to try to gauge what might be missed. Then come up with a plan to gather missed information afterward. Decide who you will ask and what you want to find out about the thing you skipped. You should validate whether or not you missed anything of relevance or importance. You may have to do this a lot at the start. You will likely kick yourself every once in a while because you did miss something. That's okay. Catch up and jump back in. Then take that learning and apply it to similar situations in the future and screen similar items for your NDL more carefully. As you get more comfortable with your NDL, this trial and error process will be faster, easier, and more routine, so this fear becomes easier to combat.

FEAR 2: FEAR OF OTHERS NOT LIKING YOU (FOONLY)

Breaking the mold of "nice and polite"

Everyone wants to be liked, included, and needed at work. Social anxiety kicks in the minute you feel like you may let someone down. It's even harder to say no to people we trust and interact with every day. Telling your colleagues, teammates, or even your boss no appears risky because it may lead to confrontation. We worry that others may not like us, include us, or think highly of us after we say no. It can frankly feel easier to sit through pointless meetings rather than confront someone about whether the meeting needs to happen. It seems easier to just keep producing the report rather than ask who is using it. It appears easier to finish the model for the client rather than tell them it's not worth building it at all. It feels easier to show up at the event rather than disappoint someone by not going. It's inherently hard to tell people no because we've been taught that nice and polite is always best. We associate being nice with saying yes. Our desire to be liked and included is like a magnet pulling us toward saying yes. It is comfortable and trusted. Going with the flow doesn't bring on social anxiety.

> OUR DESIRE TO BE LIKED AND INCLUDED IS LIKE A MAGNET PULLING US TOWARD SAYING YES.

Professionally, not everyone needs to like you; they need to respect you. How you communicate with those around you when you choose not to do something is vital to overcoming this fear. We can say no in a way that disarms others, avoids conflict, and ensures you're still respected. Later, we will cover how to decisively tell various stakeholders no, while ensuring they trust and think highly of you. As you get started building your NDL, look out for this fear. It will hold you back at first from thinking you can say no. Ask yourself whether you've avoided putting items on your NDL because of the confrontation that may result. If confrontation is the reason you hesitate to add something to your NDL, write it down anyway. You can put a star next to the item so you remember that communication techniques will be key for skipping or not doing it. The sooner you have the awkward or difficult conversations, the sooner you can move on and start winning back your time.

FEAR 3: FEAR OF LOOKING LIKE A SLACKER (FOLLAS)

Not appearing like I'm doing enough
to justify my position

Every professional has the fear in the back of their mind that they may not look as busy and productive as those around them. And no one wants to look idle or appear to not have enough work. You fear that if you don't look busy enough, then someone above you might question how you're being utilized. Or even worse, question whether you should still be employed with the organization. So what do most people do? They work late, send memos on the weekend, arrive at the office earlier than everyone else, start or join additional projects, attend more meetings, and send more FYI emails.

When you look down at your NDL and see twelve things you're going to proactively not do, naturally this fear will set in. You'll think, *If I skip all this stuff, people will think I'm unengaged and slacking off.* When you're in a constant hustle to look like you're adding value to the organization, the last thing on your mind is *What can I stop doing?*

Instead, you naturally think more, more, more will make you appear relevant and help you get ahead. More, more, more will get you a raise. The busier I am, the more value I'm adding. This is wrong. You have to flip that thinking. Leaders at your company measure results, impact, and outcomes and assess how your team, department, or division did in comparison to the targets they set. In fact, smart leaders love it even more if you can get to the same results with less effort and less running around.

This fear will kick in especially when an organization is under economic pressure. When something like the COVID-19 pandemic strikes most organizations are scrambling for cash and executing layoffs. You don't want to appear underutilized or unimportant. We try to appear "needed" by doing everything. But times of pressure, as we'll see later, are when your NDL becomes a lifeline. You must employ an NDL to ensure you focus on the few important things to achieve success personally and for the organization. Even during times of financial pressure for the organization.

As you start to build your NDL, be aware of this. Look out for activities, meetings, or events that you have traditionally gravitated toward simply to look like you're busy. Make sure to add these to your NDL. Do not live in fear of what leadership will think. Live in fear that you're not freeing up enough time to work on the extremely important value-creating activities that will propel you and your organization. Shortly, you will gain communication techniques that help explain how you're reallocating your freed-up hours to the harder things that your organization needs to solve. Having a bulletproof story about your trade-offs and being able to sell others on it is how your beat FOLLAS.

FEAR 4: FEAR OF SHAKING THINGS UP (FOSTU)

Not sticking to what we're comfortable with

People like routines. People like to not disturb the status quo. Change is not something that most people embrace quickly. It feels new, awkward, different, and potentially unsettling. But as Ginni Rometty, former CEO of IBM said, "growth and comfort do not coexist." You know going in that your NDL is going to shake things up. It's likely to dramatically change how your week looks and feels. Therefore, people avoid saying no in order to stick to the routines that are comfortable. You attend the weekly pull-up because you always have and no one else misses it. You'd rather just sit in the meeting and clear out your email. You'd rather just pull the slide together like you do every Thursday. You'd rather take the quarterly call with the client than have to cancel it.

Staying comfortable and just saying yes to everything for too long means change will eventually be forced upon you. No one likes changes forced upon them. What's unique about using an NDL is that you are driving the change. The change is not happening to you but happening because of you. You are deciding all the things to stop spending time on. You are dictating the new path for how you'll spend your precious time. You are proactively changing to stay ahead and work on harder things for your organization. Therefore, make your NDL with the understanding that you will feel much more in control of your time and outcomes. Keep reminding yourself that an NDL will bring conscious and necessary disruption to your weekly rhythm so that you can stay ahead.

FEAR 5: FEAR OF SOMETHING HARDER (FOSH)

Not being able to hide out, doing the things you're currently good at

As you go to make your NDL, you may have to cut back on things you know you're good at when you realize they are not the best use of your time. That's scary. It means you're replacing familiar things with new meetings, projects, tasks, events, and initiatives. You may not know whether you'll also be great at the new (harder) things you'll spend time on. Now, this doesn't mean you should stop spending time on everything you're good at or enjoy. Finding your strengths and playing to them is important. The point here is simple: fear will set in when we proactively choose to stop doing things that feel easy.

This fear is especially hard to overcome when you enjoy these familiar activities. You'll tell yourself, *I love meeting with that team, I'm so helpful in the market roundup, No one else can produce the report like me,* and so on. Putting these familiar items on your NDL will be hard as hell. But it's a must do in order to spend time on more difficult, unfamiliar, and important things. It's a must do to keep growing your capabilities and career rapidly. As Elon Musk stated, "you get paid in direct proportion to the difficulty of the problems you solve." Overcoming this fear requires balance and time. Don't add all your familiar (yet relatively low-value) tasks to your NDL at once. Week after week, slowly say no to more and more of the things you naturally gravitate toward. Pick more and more of the things that are not a good use of your time. You'll turn around in a few months and realize you've shifted most low-value items off your plate.

To overcome this fear, you should always have a story ready about your journey from low-value work to higher-value work. You should get credit with senior leadership for innovating and tackling harder problems. As you create and put your NDL to work, keep tabs on these shifts and the new problems you're solving. Being able to tell a crisp and compelling story about your shift toward less familiar, higher-value work will get you rewarded over time. Here are three techniques to help fight these fears.

APPLYING THE RULE OF TEN

One helpful way to overcome these fears and push yourself to add more things to your NDL, is to apply what I call the "Rule of Ten." It's quite simple. Ask yourself whether the thing you want to skip, dodge, or avoid will matter in the future. First, will it matter in ten days? Then will it matter in ten months? And finally, will it matter in ten years? Asking these quick questions will help you zoom out from your current decision and add perspective. Think about it—if you look back ten days, or especially ten months or ten years, it would be hard to point to specific meetings, distractions, events, or people that you passed up. It would be even harder to recall a specific negative event that came as a result of not doing something. These all blur into the background. However, you can likely recall the large accomplishments that happened ten days, months, or years ago. Time smooths over any choppy waters that result from not doing something you normally would. When you feel the previously mentioned fears set in, apply the Rule of Ten and remind yourself that the short-term uneasiness will be forgotten soon enough.

Constantly remind yourself that every no is actually allowing you to say yes to something more important that will get you closer to your goals.

EVISION THE END OF YOUR DAY

Here is another simpler approach to try. Close your eyes and quite literally envision being done with work and signing off for the day. Ask yourself this: will you feel better about having done the thing you know is super important or that you spent time on the low-value meeting, request, project or distraction? Stop and breathe. Assume you can't do it all and that you have to make a trade-off. Think about your potential stress level and what will make you feel more accomplished. Forecasting how you might feel will help cut through these fears and sway your decision about canceling or deleting something. Getting a taste of accomplishing the hard important things can go a long way.

RUN A PRE-MORTEM

If you're more analytical you can also try a "pre-mortem." This is a managerial strategy in which a project team imagines that a project or organization has failed, and then works backward to determine what potentially could lead to the failure. You can do the same thing for saying no. Determine what the worst outcome could be. Which of the five fears might actually come true? Ask yourself why you're truly worried. This exercise will help you understand the root fear holding you back. Then, bullet out the steps you would take to mitigate the damage. Having a plan, just incase things go poorly, will give you more confidence in reallocating your time. We're about to start building your NDL. Know that these fears will set in. Be ready with a plan to combat them.

CHAPTER 4

SHIFT YOUR MINDSET FROM YES TO NO

Say no to most things: Features. People. Partnerships.
"Coffees." Projects. Only a few of them really matter.

—EVAN WILLIAMS, COFOUNDER OF TWITTER

We'll start building your NDL in a few minutes. Let's first dive into when it makes the most sense to create and add to your NDL. The goal is to flip your mindset so you're always spotting the next no. Across the week you want to be hyperaware of other low-value items that might waste your 168 hours. We want to be constantly adding to our NDL.

MAKING AND CHECKING YOUR NOT DOING LIST EACH WEEK

Timing is everything with NDL creation. Doing it at the wrong time will create more complexity and could have a negative impact on the activities, meetings, and projects that you have going on each week. You can't decide ten minutes before a meeting that you're not going. You also can't hunt for things two weeks out because things may pop up and change between now and then. The most sustainable way to derive your NDL is in three phases each week. Spend fifteen minutes on Friday drafting your NDL for next week. Gut check your NDL on Sunday with a clear mind. And finally review and add to it every morning. Let's see how it works.

FIFTEEN MINUTES ON FRIDAY

It's Friday afternoon. You're almost ready for the weekend. But now is the time to invest fifteen minutes to save as many hours as possible next week.

Drafting the NDL on Friday afternoon is important because you have a recent perspective on what wasted your time and energy in the past five days. You can think back to pointless meetings, emails, office chats, client meetings, projects, and initiatives that ate away your precious time in the past week. These are prime candidates for what goes on your NDL for the week ahead. Having just wasted time on things will help you look forward into next week and quickly spot things for your NDL. Having your calendar open for the week ahead is important for this exercise on Fridays. We'll show you how to determine what goes on the NDL, but know that Friday afternoon is when we start. The goal is for NDL creation to only take about fifteen minutes on Friday before you sign off for the weekend. It might take you longer the first few weeks as you practice the concept.

FIFTEEN MINUTES ON SUNDAY

On Sunday nights, your mind is fresh and you are able to find even more opportunities to not do in the week ahead. Your mind has had time to relax and process what was truly important to getting ahead last week. You can lift up and assess how you're progressing toward your goals. Sunday is about making sure that anything not helping you and your organization get ahead goes on your NDL. You'll likely find more things to not do and distractions to avoid. When you made the initial list Friday, you were likely still plagued with biases from the prior week that clouded your ability to see how unimportant some recurring and upcoming events truly are. Sunday is the day of clarity to find additional items for your NDL.

AND IN THE SHOWER EVERY MORNING

Productive days don't happen by accident. Think about your average weekday morning. How does it start? Phone notifications? Email? Scrolling? The news? Checking the markets? Responding to IMs? Writing out everything you wanted to accomplish?

How you start your day is often how it will continue. Letting yourself be pulled in multiple different directions first thing can ruin your chances of getting the truly important things done.

No, the answer is not to meditate, reflect, or express gratitude. Those are helpful rituals to boost energy and center you, but they don't guarantee a productive day. To feel accomplished and in control of your time, we need to add to our NDL.

Start the day by defining what is not important and where you won't spend time. While the world is calm and still, pause and add to your NDL for the day ahead. This is your daily mini strategy session.

It only takes 5 to 10 minutes. Find a quiet place with no devices (the shower is perfect). Mentally walk through each hour. Visualize yourself in meetings, building PowerPoints, reviewing data, emailing, IMing, presenting, making lunch, coaching, sitting in one-on-one meetings, and so on. You can even describe the activities out loud.

As you do this, ask yourself these questions: Are these activities really going to get me closer to my goals? Who might waste my time or zap my energy? How might I get distracted? Where might I over-invest my time in certain activities today? Can I outsource or delegate anything I might spend time on today? If I knew 3 things wouldn't get done today, what would I choose those to be? This will help you pinpoint where the day might go off track. You want to determine upfront what will eat your time away and hold you back from the important things.

When you spot something that might be a poor use of time, make note of it. Write it down on your NDL. Do this before you start the day. Before you're pulled in multiple directions. Doing it after you check your phone, send some emails, or get into the first meeting is too late. You'll already be distracted and not focused on the right things. I do this before I even take my phone off airplane mode from the night before.

The reason this daily step is important is that throughout the flow of the week, things will pop up. This is your recurring mechanism to make sure that between Sunday and Friday, nothing creeps up and steals your time and attention.

To recap, create your list Friday, check it Sunday, and look for additional things to add on a daily basis. Now it's time to create your first NDL.

SECTION II

BUILD YOUR NOT DOING LIST (NDL)

CHAPTER 5

START WITH WHAT YOU WANT TO ACHIEVE

Focus on the things that are most important and just execute against those in a really really excellent way.

—**KEVIN JOHNSON, CEO OF STARBUCKS**

Now for the fun part. We're going to start the journey to get you more hours back each day. We'll first define your yeses, which are the things we want to spend time on. After that, we'll craft weekly headlines that will help guide your decisions about what should go on your NDL. Then we'll visit twenty-eight categories of things you should consider adding to your list and share best practices for communicating what you won't do.

One caveat before we get started. This is a framework, not a perfect process. I encourage you to iterate on it, tweak it, and make it work for you. There will be instances where it cannot be applied or certain weeks when maybe you don't need it at all. However, the more frequently we apply it and refine it, the more naturally we'll be able to focus our time and attention on the things that matter.

This all breaks down unless we first get clear on what it is that we're trying to achieve professionally. Having this clarity is key. It is what allows us to determine the relative value of all other things we could spend time on. We could call these our goals, which is defined as, the object of a person's ambition or effort; an aim or desired result. We could also call your yeses your priorities, which is defined as a thing that is regarded as more important than another.

However, building your NDL has a more specific aim, which is to help you focus. So, let's call your yeses your focus areas. Focus areas come from the world of strategic planning. Focus areas are defined as: high-priority things you plan to focus your efforts on in working toward your vision.

We will screen everything we're liable to spend time on and make sure it directly supports our focus areas. We want to make sure each meeting, project, person, event, and allowable distractions support success in your focus areas. Our focus areas serve as the guiding light for what won't get placed on our NDL. Obviously, this whole concept falls apart if we don't have a clear (short) set of focus areas. Without this we could place all the wrong things on our NDL.

SET YOUR FOCUS AREAS

For many, defining focus areas is a hard first step, and that's okay. You don't need to have a well-documented life plan to build an NDL; you just need to know the path you're on and where it leads. It could be a path for the next thirty days or thirty years or somewhere in between. For many this will be a path to your next role, a shift in responsibilities, hitting your annual goals, or success on a new initiative. Don't overthink this. This doesn't have to be your groundbreaking business idea, a big career change, or a new direction of your life. It's just where you want to focus your time in order to get closer to your next success, however you define it.

We want to get down to *three* focus areas total before we make an NDL. Yes, only three. Jim Collins, author of *Good to Great* said, "If you have more than three priorities, you have no priorities." This can't be more true on a personal level as we set off to build our NDL. With more than three focus areas, we won't find enough things to not do, because everything will still look important. This will dramatically erode the effectiveness of our NDL.

If you have focus areas clearly defined in your head or written down somewhere, great. You're in the minority and can breeze through this chapter. If not, let's create a set of focus areas now. Your focus areas for any given period should be a mix of annual performance objectives at work, new skills you're trying to build, and other professional endeavors. Let's walk through how to consider each. We will then run a quick exercise to narrow down to your three focus areas.

1. YOUR ANNUAL PERFORMANCE OBJECTIVES AT WORK

e.g., hit growth target of 8 percent, avoid risks, delight customers

Hopefully, you have these documented somewhere or can download them from your HR management system. If you don't have clear objectives or criteria in place at your organization, well, you have bigger problems that are out of the scope of this book. If goals or objectives are not readily available, work with leaders in your organization to define them. Keep in mind this is not a to-do list or a set of tasks. These are outcomes, success factors, or end-of-year milestones that you will use to measure yourself.

You need clarity about what matters in order to determine what doesn't. Without this, your NDL is essentially a shot in the dark and could actually lead to a horrible situation. If you're not confidently able to articulate the few things that will distinguish successful performance, promotion, or personal growth at work, then please don't build an NDL quite yet. If you truly can't get clarity on the big things that matter from management, take a shot at writing these yourself. Put them in front of leadership and ask them to edit and tweak them based on what they think matters most. Here are key questions you can ask yourself or discuss with leaders internally. These questions will help ensure you have clarity on what actually matters to achieving success at work this year.

> **Here are questions to ask yourself and your leadership to help get clarity on what matters to your organization and to your performance:**
>
> - What are the three things that will be used to measure success at the end of the year?
>
> - Can you rank the metrics the organization cares most about?
>
> - How can I best help the business or organization achieve its overall mission?
>
> - What allows someone to accelerate in this role quickly?
>
> - What separates performance between my current level and the next level?
>
> - What are the highest performing employees spending their time on?

2. NEW SKILLS YOU'RE TRYING TO BUILD

e.g., learn a new language, get your PMP certification, or learn to code

This one is more straightforward. Essentially, what are the skills, competencies, or knowledge that you're looking to develop. This could be a soft skill, a certification, or a new technical trade. We want to have these defined, so that the items you put on your NDL don't run counter to your development. How are you hoping to grow professionally? These are not the things you want to place on your NDL.

3. SIDE HUSTLE OR OTHER PROFESSIONAL GOALS

e.g., join a local community board, write a book, change jobs

Success against your formal work objectives and new skill development may not be all you are trying to achieve in a professional sense. Maybe you're trying to get into an advanced degree program, change careers, attain a role externally, move locations or achieve one of a whole host of other professional goals. These can be a part of your strategy or focus areas as well. These are totally valid and important things to have written down. We want to ensure your NDL clears out low-value things so you can allocate time to your other professional goals, as well.

NARROW YOUR FOCUS AREAS

After listing your work objectives, development areas, and other professional goals in these categories you may end up with a laundry list of things. Hopefully not, but most people will. A long list of focus areas is not going to get us very far because we'll end up focusing on nothing at all. Specifically, if you have too many focus areas when creating your NDL, you won't find much to say no to. When you're focused on seemingly everything, then everything will seem like a good thing to spend time on.

Again, we can have only three focus areas max when we go to create our NDL. Three. I know that's hard to do. Use this exercise to make trade-offs and get down to a smaller set of focus areas if needed.

EXERCISE: DEFINE THE FOCUS AREAS YOU'LL USE TO CRAFT YOUR NDL

First, write down your performance objectives at work, skills you're looking to develop, and other professional goals in the table here. List all relevant items, and we will then pick three total to focus on.

Annual Performance Objectives	Skills You're Trying to Develop	Side Hustle or Other Professional Goals
1.	1.	1.
2.	2.	2.
3.	3.	3.

If you're like me, coming up with three things in each category was easy. I usually have closer to seven. Now comes the hard part.

Now we need to prioritize these items in terms of what is most important. We need to get down to only three total across all categories. These three will be the focus of our time and energy. To do this, we're going to use what I call the hundred pennies exercise. Imagine you have one hundred pennies to invest. Now, allocate the hundred pennies across all the items spanning all categories. Do this based on which ones you think will get you farthest ahead throughout the next month, year, or decade. You pick the time frame. In other words, allocate your hundred pennies based on the weighting you think each of the potential items carries in the eyes of management, your income, your achievement, or however you measure success. This will give you a relative weighting for the things that matter most. This is not an easy exercise, it can't be done quickly, and it should be done on a regular basis. If you get stuck, talk to a peer, a mentor, a loved one, or even your boss about how they would weigh the various priorities you're looking at.

Look at where you allocated the most pennies. The top three will serve as your focus areas for creating your NDL. These are the three areas where we do not want to say no. These are your yeses. These are where you will invest the time you free up. You may decide to reevaluate your allocation next week or next year. It's okay if these change over time. They will absolutely change from role to role and level to level. You can update them as needed. Just remember that when one focus area gets added, you have to take one off. As things change, rewrite your articulation of what success looks like. What you use as focus areas to build your NDL can be dynamic, so if these areas change next month, simply start saying no in different places.

It doesn't ultimately matter what exercise you use to define or refine your focus areas. The point is, we need a clear list. No more than three.

The focus areas will serve as the backbone for your NDL and are what will keep it working successfully. If you're truly serious about it, print out your focus areas and tack them up at your work space or write them on a whiteboard. Make it abundantly clear how you're defining success. It's important to have these front and center at all times when you're going to start saying no left and right.

Next, we'll look at how we use these focus areas to build our NDL each week.

CHAPTER 6

WRITE WEEKLY HEADLINES TO DEFINE THE IMPORTANT THINGS YOU WILL DO

I always did something I was a little not ready to do. I think that's how you grow. When there's that moment of 'Wow, I'm not really sure I can do this,' and you push through those moments, that's when you have a breakthrough.

—MARISSA MAYER, CEO OF YAHOO

One last step before you build your NDL. Take your focus areas and translate them into a headline that captures what success looks like in the week ahead. Your headline is essentially your definition of a large positive step forward in your focus areas. It can be framed as a significant challenge or articulated as a difficult business problem you're trying to solve. It should be bold and about progress. It should also be something you're willing to run at, pretty much at any cost. The thought of your headline becoming true next week should spark joy and excitement. You should be able to look in the mirror and say, "Wow, if I could get that one thing done this week, I would feel awesome and fulfilled." A headline is vital to determining what we won't do during the coming week.

THREE FOCUS AREAS

Large measures of professional success for this year and beyond

WINNING HEADLINE

What a step forward toward your focus areas looks like this week

NOT DOING LIST

The list of what you won't do so your headline becomes a reality

An example might be "won the new business contract," "finished and submitted the proposal," "finished the research paper," "increased donations by X percent," "rebuilt a process that takes less hours for the team," or "convinced person X to work with us." Getting your headline nailed down before you start each week is vital. Your headline is what you want the newspapers to write about your accomplishments in the week ahead. The question to ask yourself is, *If I could achieve success in only one area or make progress toward one thing this week, what would it be?* Another way to think about this would be, *When I sit down for dinner on Friday night, what's the one big thing I want to feel great about accomplishing this week?* That's your headline.

Don't fall into a trap of writing what *could* happen if the week just floats by. A headline is not how your week might go. It has to define what success looks like for the coming week. You have to be comfortable that a lot of other things won't happen and won't get done in order to have your headline written. You should feel excited and happy at the prospect of accomplishing only your headline, even if nothing else at all gets done.

This headline is now your guiding light. It should bring extreme focus to what you will and won't do. Now, we need to make sure anything and everything you spend time on will help support your headline. If you foresee spending time on anything that doesn't support your headline, then it's a prime candidate for your NDL.

We're about to start building your NDL. First, two quick tips to keep in mind that will make this work.

A QUICK TEST: CAN YOU SELL YOURSELF ON DOING THE THING YOU WANT TO SAY NO TO?

We're about to dive in and review many aspects of professional life to build your NDL. You'll start thinking of things left and right to add to your NDL. But the five fears we discussed will rush in. You'll start to debate the value of each thing you place on your NDL. The default yes may win quickly if you let it. You'll think, *Should I go? Should I skip it? Should I do it? Should I not? Should I avoid this person? Maybe I have time for that,* and so on.

A quick trick to help you find a larger volume of things to not do is a practice of "selling yourself" when you get stuck. If you're debating whether something should go on your NDL, try to pitch yourself about why you *should* spend time on the potential item, not why you shouldn't do it. If you can come up with a business case for your time, then don't add that item to your NDL. But I mean a real business case. A business case tied to your headline and focus areas. A lot of the time, you'll struggle to put a pitch together to sell yourself. That's a sign you've picked something that should likely be added to your NDL. If you get stuck on a particular item, stop for a minute and try to pitch yourself. If you can't do it, well, add it to your NDL.

TAKE A ZERO-BASED APPROACH

What does zero-basing mean? Let me explain. It comes from the world of finance and relates to budgeting. The formal definition is: a method of budgeting in which all expenses must be justified for a new period. Essentially, it means starting fresh with a blank slate and using no prior assumptions. Instead of spending money on things because you "always have," it forces you to justify why every expense should be added back to the budget. Companies will start from scratch and go through each cost, line by line. They ask the question, Does this cost support growing our business? It helps you to get serious about the things that truly matter and say "no" to everything else.

We need to do the same thing with our time. Pretend for a minute that your calendar and to-do list has NOTHING on it. Literally nothing. Zero-base it. Then screen everything you might spend time to determine what is worthy of adding back. Only keep the truly important things that tie to your focus areas and headline. We want to avoid showing up on Monday and just sitting through the same meetings and completing the same activities we always would.

PRETEND FOR A MINUTE THAT YOUR CALENDAR HAS NOTHING ON IT.

Now, let's go hunting for things to put on the NDL that don't tie to your headline. The following steps are all important for winning our time and attention back in full each week. You'll notice the following steps are sequentially more and more difficult to apply. Start small with your list and aim to add more things each week as you produce your NDL.

During each step, I'm sure several ideas or examples from your life will pop into your mind. Write them down. This is your mind starting to develop the mental muscle needed to create your NDL.

CHAPTER 7

SELECT PROJECTS, MEETINGS, AND FLIGHTS FOR YOUR NDL

The difference between successful people and really successful people is that really successful people say no to almost everything.

—WARREN BUFFETT, FAMED INVESTOR

We're about visit twenty-eight categories of things you should consider adding to your NDL. We'll start with known things on your calendar in this chapter. Then we'll show you how to review your list and feel comfortable actually saying no. Each step in this section has a corresponding exercise in the appendix at the end of the book. Spend a few minutes with each short exercise to help practice looking for more things to not do. The more you practice this muscle, the more naturally you'll be able to apply it moving forward. As you learn about the items you should consider for your NDL, know that this book will also provide you with techniques to effectively communicate and defend your choices in the section that follows.

As we get started, write your headline at the top of your NDL. You can produce your NDL using the categories we're about to cover in the upcoming chapters. Alternatively, you may find it beneficial to write the things you're not going to do across days of the week (using the headers of Monday, Tuesday, Wednesday, Thursday, and Friday). As you get started, put anything and everything you think you should not do down on your list. Trust me, the five fears will kick in, and you'll still end up doing several of the things on your NDL anyway. So go big with your list. Then we can review the it. The longer your NDL is to start, the more time you'll be able to win back and allocate to things that tie to your headline for next week.

STEP 1: QUIT WORTHLESS PROJECTS

We'll start easy. Project work is easiest to assess in terms of value. The first way to win back time is stop spending it on any projects or initiatives that don't tie back to your headline. Look at your calendar, and think through the week ahead. Make sure all project work that is going to take more than thirty minutes of your time ties back to your headline. This could be the team you joined for a new initiative, working group you support, committee you sit on, presentation you were going to build, or analysis you were going to run. Are these still important to you and the mission of your company? Ask yourself if the work in question is vital to be able to write your headline for the week. If not, skip it. Write the work down on your NDL. Keep in mind, we'll screen all the potential things on our NDL at the end to make sure we're not taking too many risks. We'll also build a clear plan about how to communicate your way out of each project. Right now, we're just building the list, and we'll have time to review it. Don't let the five fears set in. Don't avoid adding things to your list. Remember how much more you can do for yourself and your organization by finding even just one hour of low-value project work that doesn't need your time next week.

STEP 2: HUNT FOR MEETINGS TO SKIP

Before you go to a new restaurant, you check the menu to make sure you'll like it. You look at the prices to make sure it's affordable. You scan the food options to make sure there are a few things you'll enjoy. You'll even read reviews and make sure other people liked it. If everything checks out, you give the new restaurant a shot. If you like the food and think it was good value for your money, you go again.

We need to start treating all meetings the same way. First, we need better visibility into what's on the menu. Second, we need to calculate the expected return on our time. Just as you wouldn't randomly walk up to a new restaurant and sit down, we need to stop doing the same with meetings.

Now, open your calendar and look across each day next week. It's likely full of various meeting invitations from a wide array of people. We need to figure out which of these you can skip, cancel, or pivot to help you achieve your headline for the week. Look at each and every one, and question, Why should I not just decline this? Read the agendas, and look at the attendees on each invite. If you don't see how a given meeting will help you write your headline next week, add it to your NDL. If there are meetings you're unsure about adding, try to sell yourself on the value. Make yourself fill in the blank to this statement: This meeting will help me with my headline by _____.

If you're more analytical, you may prefer to score upcoming meetings on a five-point scale. Fives are must attend because your boss scheduled it or it's vital to your headline. Fours will help your headline but are not vital, and so on. Scoring all meetings will force you to assign a value to every thirty- or sixty-minute block of time. This may make it easier to spot the relatively lower-value meetings, the ones you should decline.

There are exceptions to every rule; there are some meetings that require your attendance to simply help others achieve success against their priorities. A few meetings like that each week won't break your time bank, and they will help the broader organization. But you must define up front how your attendance specifically will help others be successful against their goals. If you don't have clarity about that, the meeting is a candidate for your NDL. If you need more information about a meeting, ask for it. Ask what is on the agenda or what outcomes the organizer is seeking.

You should see it almost as a sport, where you win by finding more meetings to skip each week. Make it an internal competition with yourself to see over time how many low-ROI meetings you can avoid. This should feel like shuffling cards and trying to remove the jokers from the deck. As new meetings pop up, it will feel like playing

THE WORST MEETING IS ONE WITH NO AGENDA.

a game of Whac-A-Mole, where you're continuously trying to pop the mole back into its hole. Decline meeting after meeting. The point of the NDL is to train your mind to feel good about how many hours you won back not sitting in meetings that didn't tie back to your headline or focus areas.

Challenge yourself to find at least one meeting each day next week for your NDL. Let's give it a shot. Open your calendar, and go day by day through next week. How many did you find? Ah, you're scared to actually write them down? You're probably even more scared about what could happen if you skip them. The five fears are likely setting in again. You may be thinking, *Wait, I can't skip these meetings even if they are low ROI on my time.* But you can. You should. And if you want to get ahead, you have to.

Let me share some best practices here so we can actually skip these meetings next week. I'll show you a few techniques for how to navigate your way out diplomatically as well.

There are two temptations to avoid as we start to decline meetings. First, don't just reschedule meetings. If they don't need to happen, don't kick the can down the road. Just delete it. Spending two minutes to schedule the meeting again later wastes less time than burning thirty or sixty minutes in the meeting that didn't need to happen at all. Second, don't be afraid to delete yourself off a series of meetings. Many times, we just decline the next instance of a recurring set of meetings. We do this so we can stay in the loop. If the series of meetings doesn't tie to your focus areas, decline the whole series. Saying no once is also easier than having to say no every week when you decline the next instance of the meeting. You'll thank yourself for those hours back during the weeks and months ahead.

Also, try to stack meetings back-to-back whenever possible. This will protect windows of productivity. New research from Ohio State University shows that you're 22% less productive if you know you have a meeting coming up within the next two hours.[11] Your calendar should look less like polka dots and more like a beautiful brick wall going forward.

The worst meeting is one with no agenda. These are easy candidates to add to your NDL. However not all professionals are used to crafting an agenda for their meetings. Give your colleagues a chance

---

11   Gabriela N. Tonietto, et. al., "When an Hour Feels Shorter: Future Boundary
     Tasks Alter Consumption by Contracting Time," Journal of Consumer
     Research 45, #5, February 2019, pp. 1985-1102.

to defend why the meeting should be kept in the first place. I have a standard line I send to any meeting organizer for any meeting I have coming up without a clear agenda: "What's the agenda for this meeting? Want to make sure I'm best suited to attend." Really, I'm saying, "Sell me on why this is worth my time." I tend to phrase it in a more subtle way to show that I'm still willing to take the meeting as long as there is clear alignment with what I need to accomplish. During a typical Friday afternoon, I'm pinging out this same question about an agenda to organizers of several agenda-less meetings in the coming week. And, yes, you can and should ask meeting organizers who are more senior than you about the agenda. Frame the ask in a way that is more about you preparing for the meeting. It will elevate their view of your leadership.

You should also require anyone in your reporting line to send you an agenda prior to your standing meetings together. This will ensure you and your team members run toward discussing the hard problems that need to be solved and achieve mutual success against your focus areas. This is covered in length as a best practice of high-performing managers in *High Output Management*, a business guide by Andrew Grove, chairman of the board for Intel Corporation.

Another technique to see how serious someone is about using your time wisely is to suggest a "ridiculous reschedule." Simply counter the meeting invite and suggest a new time about thirty to sixty days out. Add a line that says something like "A lot going on right now. Can we meet next month?" This is like a chess move; you want to see how they respond. It's a forcing mechanism. Seven out of ten times, they will cancel the meeting and go bother someone else. If it is important, the person will have to essentially lobby for your time. If the person has clear justification and you see how it ties to your focus areas, then you take the meeting sooner.

It's important to be on alert for new meetings that may pop up across the week or future weeks as well. As invitations roll in, your first thought should be *Why should I not just decline this?* Take a look at the new invitations you receive each day, and decline them on a rolling basis throughout the week. You don't have to wait until Friday or Monday while drafting your NDL. Declining meetings throughout the week also allows others to plan accordingly.

Another technique that might help you spot low-value meetings is to only replace meetings as new ones arrive. If a meeting invitation arrives or you schedule a new meeting, pick out a less valuable meeting to replace. Treat your calendar of meetings like your retirement account. Take a finite amount of meeting time and rebalance your hours into the best investments. This practice will churn less important meetings out of your portfolio and keep your time allocated in a smarter way going forward.

We can also flip meetings. On the surface, some meetings may not look like they align to your headline. Some meetings may look like they are a low return for your time. Don't put all of these on your NDL right away. Ask yourself if there is a way that you can influence the meeting agenda to help advance your specific goals. Instead of declining or canceling the meeting, ping the attendees and let them know you want to add agenda items that tie to your headline.

You can also attend select parts of meetings and then gain time back while attendees discuss items that won't help you write your headline. Don't sit in the meeting and try to multitask. Tell attendees you will be on for the first fifteen minutes or last thirty minutes, and get what you need accomplished. You can also start the meeting by saying, "I bet we can get to the result we need in only about fifteen minutes this morning." Doing this will challenge attendees to be brief and get to the point. You may also find creative ways to only provide a status update electronically as opposed to attending. If you can't think of any way to make the meeting tie back to your headline, then put it on your NDL.

Some meetings might appear worth your time on the surface. Then five minutes in you think, *Wait, I got tricked here; this is a total waste of my time.* Meetings might go off track, lose focus, change course, and then no longer help you write your headline. About ten to fifteen minutes into every meeting, ask yourself, *Is this still worth my time? Am I getting the return I expected?* If not, don't simply let the clock run out. Look for the next off ramp, and make a hard exit. Simply excuse yourself. Find a pause in the conversation, and say, "Hi everyone, an urgent request just hit my desk, and I need to make a call. Can someone send me the notes please?" and then drop. Trust me, at 5:30 p.m. that day, you'll pat yourself on the back for winning time back in the moment.

Also, look out for All Hands or Town Hall type meetings that will be recorded and distributed after the fact. I find that listening to these at twice the speed or at a convenient time is often a better allocation of time. You could put these on your NDL as, *Don't join town hall Tuesday at 11:00 a.m.; instead schedule time to listen to it on high speed while on a walk.*

Deploying these tactics should help you find or repurpose several meetings across your week. However, be careful of skipping the wrong meetings.

Here are meetings that should never go on the NDL:

1. Meeting with your direct manager or senior leaders in your direct reporting line

   □ *Assume that if your boss wants your time it aligns to something important. To make the best use of your time and theirs, send them an agenda proactively.*

2. High potential direct reports

   □ *Don't neglect the team members who will deliver the most toward the objectives of your team. You get the most leverage out of meeting with this employee segment.*

3. New team members during on-boarding

   □ *Prioritize time with new staff to help them ramp up. The sooner they are up to speed, the more they can produce and help you achieve success.*

4. Meetings with key customers or clients

   □ *If you're in a customer facing role, don't neglect the people writing the checks. However, also don't treat all customers equally. Segment your customers. Generate a list of customers that should never end up on your NDL. You can do this using thresholds for how much business they generate or how strategically important they are. Tier-one customers should always get your time.*

5. Meetings with contacts that are strategically important

   □ *There will be meetings that you come across with strategically important people in your organization. These should not be candidates for your NDL. Let's cover this one in a bit more detail.*

The last one is the hardest. You have to place bets about who will and who won't be important to your success down the road. These could be peers or colleagues in other functions. These are people who have influence at your organization. These are key stakeholders you'll likely work for or with throughout your career. You can still put some meetings with these individuals on the NDL, but you may want to consider your time spent with these people as an investment. Lower the threshold for the return on time just a bit knowing that you'll likely need these people as key contacts moving forward. Meetings with these people don't always have to tie back to your focus areas or headline.

You will know you're developing a winning mindset here if you open your calendar and think, *What's the next meeting I can skip?* Over time, you will treat your time for meetings like your personal budget and stop overspending in all the wrong areas.

I'll bet you're ready to start hunting for meetings to skip next week. Keep the following perspective in mind as you get going. You'll start by finding a small volume of meetings you feel confident skipping. Then as you apply the NDL framework more consistently, you'll gain confidence in skipping more meetings. You'll completely remove yourself from certain series of recurring meetings too. That means, eventually, you'll have fewer and fewer meetings that are candidates to add to your NDL week after week. That's because you'll have already eliminated so many meetings, and people will learn to stop coming to you unnecessarily. This creates a compounding effect on time savings. If your calendar eventually seems clear of low-value meetings, that's considered winning. Remember what your calendar looked like when you started using an NDL. Remember that if you had not hunted for meetings to skip each week, your calendar would still be stacked full of them. For perspective sometimes, I go back a few years in my calendar just to remember how many meetings I aimlessly attended out of habit.

It's a good reminder of how much time you're now winning back with your NDL. By week twenty-five of using an NDL, you may not find many meetings to skip. This means you're focused and reinvesting a serious amount of time into the things that matter.

If you do take a meeting, the way you enter and exit are vital. We could spend a few chapters on how to run an effective meeting. We won't. Just ask yourself, *How can I set the tone that my time is very valuable in this meeting?* When you enter, after the chitchat ceases, first make it clear that there is an agenda. Be vocal about wanting to use time effectively and what outcomes you're hoping for. Set the tone that you are not here to fill the hour, but real work needs to happen and decisions should be made. Then as you leave or close out a meeting, be clear about how you think it went and what feedback you have about how time was used. "This was a good use of time" is too vague and means nothing. When people say that, I think *Useful for who? Did we all feel that way?* Instead, leave a minute or two at the end of the meeting to ask all attendees how they would have used the time differently if the meeting was starting again. If you're short on time, shoot the attendees a quick note after. Getting feedback about the use of time in meetings will help you find more meetings to cancel and run the necessary ones more effectively.

Oh, and finally, never let a meeting run over. When you hear the deadly "Can you go over by a few minutes?" don't fall for it. First, we all know it's not just another five minutes. Before you know it, it becomes ten, then twenty, and the next full thirty-minute slot is gone in a flash. If you agree to a "few minutes," you're essentially declaring, "The next thirty minutes are wide open, and I couldn't care less if I just throw them away." Allowing this in our organization teaches people to run inefficient meetings. Instead, always give your colleagues feedback that they should reflect on the meeting and in the future pull the important sections forward so that time is better utilized. If the subject that they needed the "few" minutes to discuss is truly important, agree to consider finding more time soon.

Six questions to ask yourself about any meeting you are screening for your NDL:

1. Would my competitors sit in a meeting like this?

2. Are my customers paying me to be in this meeting?

3. Would the Board or investors applaud me for attending this meeting?

4. If someone gifted me another hour would I spend it on this meeting?

5. Will this meeting have the right attendees, data, and accountability?

6. Will I learn something valuable attending this meeting?

If you struggle to confidently answer YES, it may be wise to add the meeting to your NDL.

STEP 3: CANCEL YOUR FLIGHTS

COVID-19 turned business travel upside down overnight. Previously, professionals in client-facing roles would spend hours booking flights, cars, hotels, and meals each week and then burn several more hours on the trip itself. Now we Zoom, Skype, WebEx, or Teams with clients and prospective clients. Most professionals also had annual conferences that got wiped off their calendars in the blink of an eye. We used to go see teams in other offices and make a face-to-face connection with colleagues. Then all business travel came to a screeching halt in March 2020. Assuming it returns, we need a plan for how to screen business travel for our NDL.

Most business professionals have always conflated travel with getting work done. Most business professionals also thought seeing someone face to face was more valuable. Prior to the pandemic, how many times had you heard people say, "Oh, I'll just go see the client live," or "I need to visit my team in the Seattle office"? Or maybe you've read an Out of Office that says, "I'm at the [fill in the blank] conference this week, and my message will be delayed." If you're me, you hear or see these messages and think, *Are they really adding value or making progress against their focus areas on that trip?* When it's clear someone is conflating travel with adding value, it's tempting to interject and ask, "Are you sure that's a good use of your precious time?"

The world is different now. We all have an opportunity to press reset on how much business travel we actually do. We have an opportunity to truly evaluate the ROI on our time spent being somewhere live. In fact, COVID-19 creates the perfect set of conditions to place many trips on your NDL going forward. I know it's fun to travel. I know having drinks at the conference, squeezing in a couple of hours of beach time, or playing a round of golf is great. I know seeing a client live can be energizing and make you feel connected to customers. But time is precious. Taking the right trips is important. Taking the wrong trips can be the biggest time drain of all.

I remember talking to John, a friend, who is now a manager at a premier consulting firm based in Chicago. He told me a story about a time early in his career. A colleague suggested he go spend two weeks with his research team in India to jump-start their development on a few projects. He booked his trip a few months out. Then his division went through a sudden reorganization and he was reporting to a new leader. He told this new leader about his upcoming trip. She asked him if he had a business case to allocate eighty hours (two weeks) of his time to being on the ground in India. Never mind the sixty hours he would burn in travel alone. He said, "No, it just seems like a good idea to jump-start development on their projects." She flipped it into a return-on-time equation for him, and said something game changing. She asked, "If I gave you eighty more hours to get after your largest, most pressing goals for the year as a free gift, you're telling me this trip is for sure how you'd spend that time?" He snapped back at her, "No way." And that right there was the answer. There were much better things to spend that eighty hours on. There were things central to his headline and focus areas that should receive some of these eighty hours. He canceled the trip. Since then, John has scrutinized all live travel differently. He assesses what he could achieve with his time instead. He takes the full number of hours he would spend on a trip and assesses what he could achieve against his focus areas instead. This is how we should all screen upcoming work travel. We need to cancel the trips we shouldn't actually be taking.

We all feel the urge to see clients live, attend events and conferences, or visit another internal office. However, too often we think about the cost in monetary terms, not in terms of our time. We wonder if we can justify the expense of the flight, hotels, and meals. All in dollar terms. We often fail to think at all about the cost of our time. And time is the true cost. The cost is not being able to write a winning headline the week we travel. And it's not just the time on the plane

TIME IS THE TRUE COST.

or train. It's the time spent preparing and packing, as well as the distractions that will take place throughout the trip. We can kid ourselves that we'll work while we're there. And yes, we can get some work done on the plane. However, when I walk up and down the center aisle of any flight, there are less than 5 percent of passengers doing any real work during business hours.

There are select countries and locales where face-to-face interactions are more customary. However, you still have only 168 hours in your week. You should be willing to challenge a few customers or internal teams about the need for face-to-face meetings even in these markets. Don't default to "That client needs to see us live, because they value it and we've always done it that way." Remember that canceling even one trip a quarter will give you back precious time to work toward your goals.

Every time you go to book travel, force yourself to write a short business case. The business case should center on justifying your time, not the budget to pay for travel costs. Ask yourself, *What will I truly get out of this trip that ties back to my focus areas? What will my headline for the week be? And how will the trip help me write it?* And most importantly, tally up how many total hours the trip will cost you in terms of time. Is there *really* nothing else with a higher return you should spend those hours on? Imagine winning back dozens or even hundreds of hours in a year and reallocating them to the things that are hard and tie to your focus areas. Don't put business at risk, but always make yourself write a business case for your time. This will help you determine which trips you should and shouldn't take.

Travel is fun. It's hard to be honest with yourself. You won't skip all trips. We all need a little change of pace and time out of the office here and there. But if you can find a few trips a year to put on your NDL, you should. Those precious hours could make or break your ability to successfully hit your objectives for the year.

On a tactical note, putting trips on your NDL requires more foresight than just looking at the week ahead. Realizing on Friday that you should cancel a three-day trip the following week is not great for customers or your travel costs. By then, you have likely lost time preparing and planning for the trip. Remember to screen these trips prior to booking them. When you catch yourself punching airport codes into the search engine, stop and ask yourself, *When that week comes around, will I feel like this is the best use of my time?*

STEP 4: BLOCK THE REST OF YOUR CALENDAR

In the steps thus far, you've freed up (hopefully) a lot of time across the week. Now, block enough time on your calendar to execute the important task(s) that tie to your focus areas and headline. As mentioned earlier, you don't need a to-do list in addition to your NDL. You should take the items that would be on your to-do list and create private calendar appointments for yourself. Block enough time to do the important things well. Schedule a meeting with yourself where real work gets done. This self-meeting is just as important as a meeting with others. If we leave space open on our calendars, we're inviting people to steal it. Someone who doesn't understand the value of time may see your unscheduled "free space" and think you have nothing important to get done.

Blocking your calendar is vital to making your NDL work. When you cancel or decline a meeting, book a replacement meeting with yourself during that slot. Look out across the week ahead, and fill in all free space with self-meetings to get hard work done. Block time in the morning to get your most strategic work done before distractions takeover. Also, block enough time for routine activities each day such as email. More on these topics shortly. This should feel like paint by numbers, where we need to color in every inch of our calendar. You can even use your weekly headline as the title for your self-meetings. This will show people what you're focused on. Others will be less likely to try to steal your time if they see a three-hour block on your calendar titled, "Negotiate Five Year Contract," or "Enhance Business Pipeline for Q4," or "Redesign Global Process Flow." When colleagues look at your availability, they will see important things and little-to-no free space. They will respect that time more than if your calendar appears wide open. These blocks are key to writing your headline and ending each week feeling in control.

Now, let's get into how we should view the people we interact with across the week. We can also add some of them to our NDL.

CHAPTER 8

NAME COLLEAGUES, CUSTOMERS, AND UNDERPERFORMERS FOR YOUR NDL

If you want to make everyone happy don't be a leader—sell ice cream.

—STEVE JOBS, FORMER CEO OF APPLE

As we dive into the next section, do yourself and the world a favor. Break the following rules if it helps empower and lift up minority voices in your organization. We'll look at this more closely when we pressure-test your list, but please have that in mind as you review the upcoming chapter.

STEP 5: DODGE THE ENERGY VAMPIRES

Nike was founded on ten business values that allowed the leadership team to rapidly build a world-leading brand. One of those values relates to a list of dangers that can stall the organization and must be avoided at all costs. One of these dangers was framed as "energy givers versus energy takers." Here, we're going to use our NDL to proactively spot any energy takers and dodge them.

You know the type. The people you dread catching up with. The people who either waste your time or waste your energy. Or both. They just burn their time away complaining, making things harder, or coming up with excuses. They are often rude or uncooperative or don't care, and as a result sap your motivation and ability to get things done. When you meet with these people, you feel exhausted and rarely get anything actually accomplished. You feel deflated. I bet a few people are coming to mind. These are energy vampires.

Adding these people to your NDL is extremely freeing. We won't be able to dodge them all, but avoiding interactions with even a few energy vampires each week can be game changing. Getting this right will not only get you back time but also help you stay positive and maintain your energy levels. The concept of energy vampires comes from the work of Christiane Northrup, MD, in her 2018 book, *Dodging Energy Vampires: An Empath's Guide to Evading Relationships That Drain You and Restoring Your Health and Power*. She discusses the phenomenon of energy vampires and shows readers how to spot them, dodge their tactics, and take back your own energy. She highlights how vampires use others' energy to fuel their own dysfunctional lives. Her work focuses on the totality of the relationships in your life: family, friends, and anyone you may come into contact with. From a professional standpoint, there is no better place to put the energy vampires than onto your NDL. We must spot them, name them, and be ready to dodge them at every turn.

In 2004, Tom Rath published a number-one *New York Times* Best Seller, *How Full Is Your Bucket?* Fifty years of research that went into the book reveals how even the briefest interactions affect your relationships, productivity, health, and longevity. Rath poses a question about every interaction we have: "Did that person—your spouse, best friend, coworker, or even a stranger—'fill your bucket' by making you feel more positive? Or did that person dip from your bucket, leaving you more negative than before?" According to the theory, each person has a bucket and a dipper. With positivity, you fill your bucket and the buckets of others. With negativity, you deplete others' buckets as well as your own. Dodging energy vampires is about protecting your bucket by simply saying no. You are proactively deciding who you will not let dip from your bucket by placing them on your NDL. Letting someone steal your positive energy could severely impact your ability to write a winning headline that week.

Let me give you an example. An applications manager at a Fortune 100 consumer-goods company was recently complaining about a colleague who works alongside her on a peer team. She described Nick. She said he just babbles on, gets very little accomplished, can't focus, and likes to hear himself pontificate about uncontrollable challenges in the organization. She explained that he'll often just pop by or show up and bring around negative vibes. "Nick just drains all my energy. Makes me deflate. Makes me the opposite of excited to work on the hard challenges for our business."

I asked her if she needed to work with Nick to achieve success on her focus areas. She said, "I think so; I always have. He just always says 'it's important' to pull up and get updates every other week, so we do." I challenged her to write out exactly what she was getting from Nick that she could not be successful without. Like really, honestly, anything that Nick was providing that was truly vital to her success. She was drawing a blank and said, "I guess, nothing really." I coached

HAVING SOMEONE DRAIN AWAY YOUR MOMENTUM AND ENERGY WILL COST YOU A LOT.

NOT DOING LIST

her to immediately put him on her NDL. I told her, "Put his name, Nick, specifically on your NDL. He's what you're 'not doing' this week. Make it a point to specifically dodge him. Cancel any meetings with him. If you see him in the café, walk the other way. Put him on the NDL and celebrate the escape of this energy vampire."

I'm sure you have a few energy vampires in your organization too. It's bad when people waste your time. It's even worse if they also drag you down or divert your attention to the wrong things. Having someone drain your momentum and energy will cost you a lot. Spending an hour with an energy vampire is not only a waste of an hour; it can set you back for the rest of the day. They can drain your power, distract your focus, and put you at risk of not having a winning headline for the week.

In a CNBC interview in 2019, Brian Niccol, the turnaround CEO of the fast-casual growth company, Chipotle, discussed his philosophy on hiring managers across his employee base. He uses what he called "the hallway test." It's quite simple. He shared that he wants to hire only managers he enjoys seeing in the hallway, not those that you "want to duck into a conference room to avoid."[12] This is similar to the notion of dodging an energy vampire. Don't associate with or hire employees that you want to hide from because you know they will steal your time, energy, and attention.

Pinpoint these people. Keep them on your NDL. If you forecast running into them, go the other way to avoid them. If they try to grab time with you, fight it off like the plague. Don't join projects with them. If they end up on your team, put them on a performance

---

12 "CNBC's Kate Rogers Interviews Chipotle Mexican Grill CEO Brian Niccol from the CNBC Evolve Conference in Los Angeles Today," CNBC, November 19, 2019, https://www.cnbc.com/2019/11/19/cnbc-transcript-cnbcs-kate-rogers-interviews-chipotle-mexican-grill-ceo-brian-niccol-from-the-cnbc-evolve-conference-in-los-angeles-today.html.

plan with HR and get them out the door. Don't try to fix them. Your precious time needs to be allocated to much higher return areas so you can keep advancing.

Your NDL should have either the names of the energy vampires or the specific events and projects with those vampires that you will not do. The hard part about this is that at certain moments you may feel bad or want to avoid conflict with them. Never feel bad. You may even want to coach and fix them. Don't. Don't spend time trying to get them to improve. These people will glob on to someone else and drain their time and energy soon enough.

If you absolutely can't say no to an energy vampire, limit your interaction with them or meet with them at the very end of the week so they don't kill your vibe. Also, importantly, make it known in any performance feedback to their manager. Explain how this person limits your ability to get important things done because they are a taker of energy, not a giver. Remember that removing these individuals was key for Nike to transform from selling shoes in a garage to a Fortune 500 company.

STEP 6: REFUSE TO HELP ROLE JUSTIFIERS

We've all heard of make-work, or work assigned or done chiefly to keep one busy. It's work that does not necessarily support growth and profitability. As companies grow and mature, a percentage of staff and work will fall into this bucket. We need to dodge this work, and our colleagues who are doing this type of work, with our NDL. We must stay focused on work critical to the success of our organization. Those conducting primarily make-work are essentially trying to justify their role. We'll call them role justifiers here.

Let's start with why we end up with role justifiers in our organization. We hire people into roles when there is a critical volume of work or a leader needs to justify their scope. Then things change, and the person who was hired is left trying to justify their role. Organizations also go through growth spurts and bring on a large number of staff, only to then have slower growth. This leaves some of those hired trying to justify their role. Reorganizations happen, and people are moved into functions they know little-to-nothing about and are then left trying to justify their role. Leaders hire staff for a specific job and then move on, leaving staff trying to justify their role. The core work an organization does will sometimes dry up or change in nature, and the people hired are then stuck trying to justify their role. This ebb and flow of talent is a constant for most organizations today. We live in a world with very inflexible labor models where it is difficult to terminate staff stuck in these situations. These individuals can end up running around the organization getting people involved in the next "important" project. They stir up work that doesn't really need to happen. They build processes around things that don't need any attention. They standardize workflows that don't have any issues to being with. They look for ways to expand initiatives that are no longer mission critical. As they sputter, they leech on to those who will spend time with them. The larger the organization, the larger this problem usually is. It's also pervasive at unfocused organizations. Too often, they have people in roles where they don't actually need the people, but it's too much effort or risk to get rid of them.

This, then, poses a problem for you. Those trying to justify their role will email, call, and IM you and try to divert your time and attention away to their make-work. With every request, we must stop and consider: is this mission-critical work or make-work? Do not pay any attention to the make-work requests. Write the names of role justifiers and their make-work down on your NDL, and refuse to spend time with them. As you progress through the leadership ranks, deploy these individuals to mission-critical work or remove them from the organization. Each week you should have a list of three to five of these people you will not let tug you away from what's important. We'll show you how to tell role justifiers no in a subsequent chapter, but for now let's name them and get them on our NDL.

It might look as simple as this on your NDL:

- Tyler in content promotion

- Sam in outbound production

- Rakim in facilities

- Olli in sales operations

You may also realize that you have role justifiers on your own team. There are two ways this happens. First, the nature of the work changes on your team, and certain individuals can't perform or their work is no longer required. Find them a new role. Do not let these individuals linger because they will sap time from you and other colleagues. Other leaders may also try to gift you talent. This is when someone proactively gives you a new staff member without you having screened them. Another leader says to you, "Good news, we're going to move Jeni and Carlos onto your team next month. I'm sure you can put them to work!" When you're gifted talent, you don't get the opportunity to screen these staff members for the critical competencies you need. You also don't get to ensure that you have adequate work for them. These individuals can then become role justifiers very quickly. This again will drain your time. All leaders should stop immediately when they receive a gift and make sure they are not bringing role justifiers onto their team.

STEP 7: STOP DOING OTHERS' WORK

Many organizations today are working to break down silos and drive cross-functional collaboration. For certain situations this can help various departments collaborate, increase the speed of decision making, and hold people jointly accountable. Bluntly, it can also mean that you end up doing someone else's hard tasks, while they sign off at 5:00 p.m. to watch Netflix.

I was at a café in Buenos Aires with Bob Sicina, former President of Latin America and the Caribbean for American Express, when he shared an important lesson with me. We were waiting (not so patiently) on the check and running late to a client meeting. We asked the waiter for the check for the third time. The waiter said, "The machine is down right now; it will be about twenty minutes." Bob said in a soft, calm, and firm voice, "There are two kinds of problems in life—'your problem' and 'my problem.' Don't let your problem become my problem." The waiter paused and thought about it. He knew Bob was right. He grabbed a napkin and handwrote our bill. We were out of there in three minutes.

Bob's framing of "my problem" and "your problem" carries over to the daily flow of work in most professional settings. We must get clear on what "my" problems to solve are and are not. In the current fast-paced environment, we too often start solving problems and assigning next steps, and before we know it, we've actually agreed to solve someone else's issue or challenge. Now, of

WE MUST GET CLEAR ON WHAT "MY" PROBLEMS TO SOLVE ARE AND ARE NOT.

course we want to be strong corporate citizens and help work toward collective goals. But when we take on the responsibility to work on something or solve a problem, we must be clear on whether or not it's our problem to solve. We must stop and ask ourselves, "That thing I'm about to spend an hour on—is that really my problem or should someone else own this?" If somehow, the "problem" was volleyed across the organizational matrix and landed in your lap, it should be considered for your NDL. Start by solving "my problems," and then if you have capacity, you can lean in and help others solve their problems.

There are also times when we find ourselves inadvertently doing routine or process-related tasks that should be owned by others around the organization. We create shadow systems of record, we build the marketing fliers ourselves, we end up engaging with someone else's client, we support IT testing, and we train other teams. Now, this is not to say we shouldn't be helpful and support the broader goals of the organization. But we should know when we're doing our work versus someone else's work. We must draw the line somewhere. It's on us to make sure we draw that line at all. Your NDL is the tool to define where we will stop substituting for others around the organization.

As you screen the activities you have coming up next week, look for tasks, meetings, and processes that really should be owned by others. Instead of just executing these out of habit, determine who should own them and reassign this work to the right individuals. This is harder in some organizations, especially where lines of ownership are blurred. We don't need to redefine work processes for the entire organization to find quick wins on this front. Find one thing each week to send back to its proper owner, and hold yourself accountable for not doing it yourself with your NDL.

You might be thinking, "yeah, but if I give this work back to the correct owner then it won't be done correctly or on time." This might be true. But, for us to focus our time and energy on solving bigger more important problems we need to expose this fact and work on finding longer-term solutions. It's your job as a leaders to expose failure. We can't band-aid over the inadequacy of others and run a more successful organization. By exposing failure we highlight the problem and make it known where we've been substituting. Now, we can't just throw these items on our NDL next week. Acknowledging that this is even happening is a big first step to resolving the issue. Then, we must work with leaders internally and provide ideas for longer-term solutions. Help find a sustainable alternative and slowly shift these items onto your NDL.

Those who change internal jobs frequently will run into this challenge quite often. As you move from role to role at the same company, colleagues will still revert to asking you for support on things you no longer own. You will still be tagged to legacy project plans, org charts, and processes. As you move to a new role internally, you must break free and give your prior work back to the new owner in that role. Use your NDL as a way to define when and how you will let go of former tasks in order to excel in the new role you moved into.

This also is important for leaders to remember as they progress into management roles. You have to stop doing the work, and start developing your team to run without your involvement. Tim Ryan, US chair and senior partner at PwC said in a 2020 interview on the podcast *How Leaders Lead*, "In your first several years, you can do a lot yourself. Then you come to the realization you can't do it all yourself. There were times when I was working around the clock because I felt this insecure need to do everything myself and get it done right. You can do that at one level, but by the time you get to certain levels, your responsibilities become so big that if you don't learn to trust others and give them guidance to show you what they have, then you will hit a ceiling. I've seen hundreds and hundreds of people hit a ceiling because they can't get over that comfort level."[13] Your NDL is a tool that you can use to make this leap. Put down on your NDL the things you know your team should own, and commit to not stepping in and doing it for them. Say no, win back time, and up your leadership profile.

STEP 8: DECIDE WHO HAS TO ASK YOU TWICE

A former colleague took a manager role in sales at a large healthcare company a few years ago. I asked him how internal operations worked compared to his former employer. He described the internal processes for getting what he needed from the procurement function. He said, "It's kind of odd; they never respond until I email them a second time." He went on to share, "It's kind of brilliant, because they find out who really needs their time and support to solve their problem." He said, "There is a lesson in having people ask you twice. Not everyone, but some people should have to ask again." He told me that he started taking the same approach with certain clients and colleagues. He said it drastically freed up his time and focused him on the things people really needed.

His procurement function at the healthcare company was using a Service Level Agreement (SLA). SLAs have emerged as commonplace in business for most internal functions like finance, HR, marketing, risk, and legal. These agreements are simply rules of the road for how

---

13 David Novak, "Leading with Guts: PwC US Chair & Senior Partner Tim Ryan," 2020, How Leaders Lead, podcast, https://podcasts.apple.com/us/podcast/leading-with-guts-pwc-us-chair-senior-partner-tim-ryan/id1223803642?i=1000494011969.

these internal functions will provide support to the organization. The agreement defines what services they will provide, who will provide them, when they will provide the services, and how they will deliver those services. It helps these functions manage time and workflow. It allows them to provide consistent, high-quality, well-timed support to the rest of the company. They budget their time and people in order to deliver against the service agreements set out with teams around the organization.

What if you could act in the same way as an individual? What if you had an SLA with certain colleagues about what you would provide and how quickly? What if you predefined how much time you would spend on certain tasks for certain people? What if you knew that for a certain process, task, or person you would not respond in less than seventy-two hours? What if you could create a list of people you were okay not responding to for a week? What if you created a list of people you would make ask you twice for something before you respond?

WHAT IF YOU PREDEFINED HOW MUCH TIME YOU WOULD SPEND ON CERTAIN TASKS FOR CERTAIN PEOPLE?

You can. And you should. Think about all the informal agreements you have with people to get work done already. Predefining how much support you're willing to provide up front should be part of your NDL. Defining who has to ask twice should be part of your NDL as well. When you get the request from that person, delete it until they follow up.

This is different from the energy vampires or role justifiers, who you'll dodge completely. An SLA is for work and individuals whose focus and intent is justified because they are supporting mission-critical work. An SLA simply helps you put a fence around the specific task, speed, and quality you're going to provide for them up front. You're setting ground rules to avoid letting the loudest or most needy colleagues distract you or steal your time.

The SLA with these colleagues doesn't need to be actually agreed upon with them. You're agreeing on it with yourself. You may need this type of agreement for only a few colleagues. It is most helpful to have in place for those colleagues who come to you frequently and seem to always want more of your time. It could also be helpful for colleagues who seem to always change what they need from you or those who want something requiring more effort each time. Those who always request more data, more examples, more views, and a different format.

Beyond making someone ask twice, you can also simply slow your response or give them only the minimum level of support. Your NDL is a mechanism to help you not budget any more time than necessary for supporting these individuals. You're committing up front to spend only X amount of time on thing Y for person Z. An example might be "I will spend only twenty minutes on updating the client data for Nathan this week" or "I will not add any new pages to the process review deck this month" or "when Jara pings me, I won't respond for five hours to see if she can solve the problem herself." You're simply putting a stake in the ground up front about where you won't allocate any additional time or effort. Defining this each week for select colleagues is liberating. You're using this section of your NDL to declare where you won't overinvest.

Here are a few examples of what this might look like on your NDL:

- Make Rick, Symone, Jim, Liz, Harsha ask twice for any support this week

- Don't respond to marketing about the client interviews for seventy-two hours

- Don't send full model back to Darnell (a draft this week is fine)

- Don't create a detailed process map for Liz; send her bullets instead

- Don't send Robert a preread deck for the meeting

You can take this a step further and create various levels of support. Gold, silver, and bronze, for example. Decide who gets your gold level of support, which might be instant, high quality, anytime. Decide who gets bronze, which might be delayed or bare-bones and the person has to ask you twice. Use your NDL as the process to write down who is in the bronze category this week.

You know where you'll overserve someone and provide more than is required or respond faster than someone actually needs. The idea here is that you proactively spot where this might happen and write it down. Give yourself credit and a pat on the back at the end of the week for not overserving anyone. Those hours need to be spent in a much more valuable way.

STEP 9: FIRE YOUR LEAST PROFITABLE CUSTOMERS

Not all customers are created equal. Some bring you more revenue. Some bring you less revenue. Some are easy to work with; others are difficult to please. Spending time with some customers will always yield new leads. Spending time with others will feel like you're beating your head against a wall. Some customers overuse your time relative to what you earn from them. Some underuse your time relative to what you earn from them. If you're in a customer facing role, understanding these differences about your customers is key. You have to be able to allocate your time, attention, and focus to maximize total revenue and reduce total time (or resources) needed to generate that revenue. "Let your time follow the easy money," as one sales executive put it.

We've all met the superneedy client. Everything seems like an emergency. They needed everything yesterday. They want special terms and a more tailored product. Too many of these clients can harm the organization's profitability and lead you to burnout. They can steal your time away from other current and future clients. Every minute lost with this type of customer is holding you back from earning more revenue from another customer. This is why you have to proactively manage these clients using your NDL. This will be unique to your position and the distribution and diversity of your organization's client base. If your client base is highly concentrated, this is harder. You should put your least profitable client relationships on your NDL, as long as the revenue from losing that particular client won't meaningfully harm total revenues. If the client is material to your organization's overall business health, then that client (needy or not) may be something you are prioritizing time for, not putting on your NDL.

When a relatively immaterial client is potentially going to waste your time and erode your focus, you need to proactively make it known that you have boundaries. You must consider if you need the client at all. Do you need to actually "fire" your client in order to focus on others? There is a certain percentage of clients that will cause more harm (in wasted time and lost focus) than their revenue is actually worth. If you sense this, I'd raise this with others internally. Ask your colleagues for their opinions about whether you should just let the business go. Again, this could be vital in order to focus your time and energy on more profitable or larger revenue clients.

DO YOU NEED TO ACTUALLY "FIRE" YOUR CLIENT IN ORDER TO FOCUS ON OTHERS?

The clients you don't fire, those you keep, should still be screened. Determine what you don't need to do to get to the same resulting revenue. In short, you will still want to be on the hunt for requests, projects, meetings, and events across your client base that you can add to your NDL.

When you go to make your NDL for the coming week, think about which customers are likely to be unprofitable in the weeks ahead. Decide if your time is worth the potential return (i.e., the revenue they bring to your organization). Pick 5 to 10 percent of your least profitable customers from a return-on-your-time standpoint, and put them on your NDL. This is hard if you're in a sales territory that needs every dollar to count, but even saying no to the least profitable customers will let you reinvest that time into growing your more profitable accounts.

STEP 10: PICK BATTLES TO LOSE

We often find ourselves in heated discussions with colleagues through-out the normal course of any week. We could be debating product features, communication plans, process changes, data to collect, reporting we should do, customers we should chase, or a plethora of other topics. We must know when to keep fighting for our approach and when to lose and move on. At times, we get so caught up in needing to be right that we burn hours trying to win every debate or have our ideas accepted. We can't always win, and we don't have to in order for us and our organization to be successful.

As you build your NDL for a given week, play out different scenarios where battles and debates with colleagues will emerge. Decide up front, with your limited time, where you will wage war and where you will not engage entirely. Forecast where you will rumble with colleagues on a better approach and where you will leave it up to others to make the call. This is vital to making sure you don't throw your time away. Your NDL helps you get comfortable deciding where not to engage. It helps you avoid the *winning at all costs* mentality for decisions that don't need that approach. Find the potential battles that you are okay to lose and place them on your NDL as a reminder not to wage war.

When something unexpectedly pops up or goes sideways midweek, you may become heated. Someone dropped the ball on something. Someone went back on their word. Someone changed course without telling you. Someone posed a risk they shouldn't have. When fired up in the moment about this, you can sometimes forget how precious your time is. You may drop what you're focused on to draft an angry response or call someone to make your opinion known. We shouldn't do that. We should pause, breathe, and ask whether we really care. Decide if you will still care in ten days, ten months, or ten years. Don't try to win every battle. Instead of immediately channeling your anger and throwing away your time, pause and decide whether we should just let it go by placing it on our NDL. Find peace in the fact that you didn't burn time battling with someone on something that really doesn't matter at the end of the day. Of course, if it is important to win the battle and have your voice heard, find the right time and venue to do that. Hopefully after you have cooled off and are levelheaded.

DECIDE IF YOU WILL STILL CARE IN TEN DAYS, TEN MONTHS, OR TEN YEARS. DON'T TRY TO WIN EVERY BATTLE.

Changes to people, processes, and systems also raise anxiety and put us in battle mode. When we hear about a change, we ask questions like, Why? Who made the decision? and Shouldn't we consider another approach? Throughout any year there will be new policies, new central mandates, new websites, new technology applications, new CRMs, additional processes, amended procedures, and added checks and balances to your workflow. The pace of these changes is only becoming more rapid. Many professionals burn their time trying to fight back on these changes, give their opinion, or explain why there is a better approach. At established organizations, you could spend your whole day fighting back against all the new things that get rolled out. Please don't. Instead, reinvest that time into your focus areas.

When you notice yourself getting angry or agitated about a new change, stop and first decide if you can influence the outcome. Then determine if influencing the change will lead to more rapid success against your focus areas. If not, then choose to lose the battle against the change. Instead of firing off the angry email or tossing your time out the window complaining about the change, commit to not spend time fighting back using your NDL. Decide to lose the fight with the change. Give yourself credit on your NDL for rolling with the change and operating within the system. This doesn't mean you shouldn't speak up and help your organization operate more efficiently. We just can't throw away precious hours trying to preserve the status quo. You decide for yourself the percentage of time you can and should use to try to influence any changes that are being rolled out. Even picking a few battles to lose each month could get you back multiple hours for your focus areas.

Next time you start to get heated, stop and ask yourself if this is a battle you simply will choose to lose with your NDL. You can't win them all.

STEP 11: SCRUTINIZE SERVICE PROVIDERS TRYING TO "HELP"

Professionals, regardless of seniority, are inundated with service providers trying to sell information, data, networking, education, or a host of other support and resources. Some of these services are vital to our success and well worth the monetary cost. However, usually the true cost of engaging with these service providers is your time. When you meet with these service providers, you should analyze the time investment, not just the price tag. The dollar cost can be recouped. Your time is gone forever.

First, before you answer the phone or read their email, know clearly what problems you're trying to solve. If you don't know that, then you'll be sold a solution looking for a problem. The problems to solve should tie back to your focus areas, work objectives, and headlines. Next, understand the true cost in terms of your time. Focus on understanding the time investment required to get the value you need. If you have to burn fifty hours working with a service provider to get value, then the true cost is the lost opportunity of how you could otherwise spend those hours. When you make your NDL for the week, decide which service providers you won't spend time with. Pick those that don't solve your real problems or are not worth the time investment. Decide which calls and offers you'll decline. Put the names of these service providers down on your NDL and dodge them going forward.

STEP 12: SCALE BACK TIME WITH UNDERPERFORMERS

Research from global staffing firm Robert Half shows that managers spend more than ten hours "coaching underperforming employees" during the average workweek. That's 26 percent of business hours.[14] This step is about deciding when to stop making that investment and reallocate this time.

If you're in a management role, nothing is more important than your team. You have to take care of the climate and build trust. You have to motivate people to perform and achieve their goals. As a manager, you also can't accept underperformance. It's frustrating, time-consuming, and can demoralize the other people on your team. You have to make a conscious choice about which team members will get your time and attention. You cannot spend the same amount of time with each member of your team, nor should you. Don't spread your time like peanut butter across your team. There is a multiplier on your time as a manager. Spending time with the right team members

---

14   Jane Burnett, "Survey: Managers spend 26% of their time coaching bad employees," Ladders, May 16, 2018, https://www.theladders.com/career-advice/survey-managers-spend-more-than-10-hours-a-week-on-poorly-performing-employees.

can grow your impact. The wrong ones will diminish it. Even if you're not in a dedicated management role, the following still applies. This is how you should think about which team members you will and, more importantly, won't spend as much time with.

Most managers spend their time trying to get everyone to be a great employee. Many think their time is best spent fixing those who are struggling or not performing as well. They run toward giving lower performers feedback and building development plans for employees who are off track.

MANAGERS SPEND MORE THAN TEN HOURS "COACHING UNDERPERFORMING EMPLOYEES" DURING THE AVERAGE WORKWEEK.

Spending some time with these members of your team is justified, but only to a point. You have to know when to draw the line and when these team members won't get back on track. Allocating too much of your time to underperformers can hold you back from other, more important, segments of your team. If week after week your time is being spent with employees that fall into the underperforming category and you're not seeing rapid improvement, consider putting these employees on your NDL. Decide when you've invested enough time trying to get someone back on track and they simply can't do it.

You can't ignore or avoid these members of your team forever. We can't let them drain resources for long. We have to find a solution for them. First, make sure you're giving these employees a fair chance and all the resources they need to exhibit the competencies and achieve the goals you have set out for them. Then make sure that these employees hear from you directly that they are underperforming and also not improving. Next, consider moving them to another team that might be a better fit, working with them to find another role, or helping them to exit the organization. Tough conversations with someone about not meeting performance expectations should *not* go on your NDL. Have the tough conversations as soon as you can. As they look for a new role, use your NDL to make sure you don't overinvest time with them each week.

On the contrary, there are three segments of your team that will positively multiply the impact of your time. First, pinpoint who on your team is a high performer, or roughly the top 20 percent of your team in terms of performance. Second, look for high potential employees, those who you feel will achieve high performance with the right coaching and development. Third, make sure you know who is new to the team and ramping up to speed. Make sure meetings and support for these three groups rarely end up on your NDL. Enable high performers to keep achieving more by providing direction and removing roadblocks. High potentials need your coaching and feedback to keep reaching to the next level of performance. Prioritize helping new members of your team to reduce the time it takes to have them up and running. We also want these new team members to feel supported and get critical feedback early. Time spent with new employees will help them operate independently with a full workload more quickly.

The more time spent with these three groups, the faster you'll achieve collective team success. Don't avoid the weekly one-on-ones with individuals in these three groups. Don't say no to helping them overcome setbacks. Respond to their emails first. Don't not review their work or not give them feedback. Don't put their projects on your NDL. It's easy to think, *Oh, they've got it; they don't need my time.* Wrong. You want to spend time with these three groups as a priority. Take a look back through your NDL and make sure these three groups are not on it. You'll erode trust and drastically hurt your chances of running a successful team.

Not sure who on your team falls into the high-performer or high-potential bucket? Ask yourself a tough question: If the economy fell off a cliff tomorrow and you could keep only a small percentage of your staff, who would it be? These are the employees we want to invest the most time with. These are the ones we should not have on our NDL. Now, of course, we will and should spend some time with team members in the middle of the pack. But not as a priority. Time spent on meetings, projects, reviews, and other work with employees in the middle of the performance pack should be screened just like everything else.

To recap, put low performers on your NDL, while at the same time finding a way for them to exit the organization if they are not improving their performance. Do not put high performers, high potentials, or the newest employees on your NDL. Your time has a high return on investment in helping these three groups succeed. Screen activities with employees in the middle of the pack for your NDL using the other steps we've covered.

CHAPTER 9

ADD INFORMATION, PROCESSES, IDEAS, AND ROUTINE TASKS TO YOUR NDL

The question I ask myself like almost every day is, 'Am I doing the most important thing I could be doing?'… Unless I feel like I'm working on the most important problem that I can help with, then I'm not going to feel good about how I'm spending my time.

—MARK ZUCKERBERG, CEO OF FACEBOOK

If you take a step back and think about how many pieces of information we consume each day, it's astounding. We are inundated with sports scores, stock prices, dashboards, articles, threads, meeting notes, tweets, and PowerPoint decks packed full of data in ten-point font. There are currently 2.5 quintillion bytes of data created each day, and it's only accelerating with the growth of the Internet of Things (IoT). In a 2018 article Bernard Marr states that 90 percent of the data in the world was generated in the previous two years.[15] The problem is time. We don't get more time. Our minds have a vast amount of brainpower and can compute more information than we would ever have time to consume. Leaders who prioritize the right information will be those who pull ahead in our fully digital workplace. Your NDL is where you commit to screen out the right data and information and feel good about ignoring it. The following steps teach you how to place bets on which information and data will drive you and your organization forward and say no to the rest.

STEP 13: DELETE DATA AND INFORMATION

In a world with more data and reports flying into your inbox, you will be tempted to try to review everything you receive. You will fear that something may be lurking in the data that you might miss. This is risky. You don't have time to burn, and we can't treat everything equally. Now, of course, data and information are vital to sound decision making. Don't mistake that. However, to get ahead in a digital world, we have to be selective and focused about what we consume. We need to recognize patterns in our information consumption and identify when we repeatedly don't find anything useful.

We have all been in the situation where the data or notes land in our inbox for a given project. We spend twenty minutes poring over them, trying to find anything meaningful. We think, *Well, I guess if someone asks, I can say I reviewed it.* However, most of the time, we

---

15   Bernard Marr, "How Much Data Do We Create Every Day? The Mind-Blowing Stats Everyone Should Read," Forbes.com, May 21, 2018, https://www.forbes.com/sites/bernardmarr/2018/05/21/how-much-data-do-we-create-every-day-the-mind-blowing-stats-everyone-should-read/?sh=6d00c70560ba.

find nothing that helps us make progress toward writing our headline. We're consuming information just in case there is something of value. A lot of the information we receive is recurring in nature as well. We see it on a similar cadence. We check the same apps, open the same emails, or receive the same sets of data each month. Sure, we can encourage senders to call out the important trends or insights. That does help. However, the questions we need to be asking are, What am I able to really do with this information? How does it help me make progress toward my focus areas? If you find that you're consuming data or written information out of habit, then you should pause and ask why? We must also ensure we trust the source before we blindly consume data and information.

This is where your NDL comes in. We must make a conscious effort to proactively decide which information is likely not necessary and delete it. In fact, we don't even have to delete it; we can stick it in a folder somewhere. We just have to commit to not spend time blindly consuming ALL data and information that we receive.

Think about when you are likely to spend time consuming data and information in the coming week. Will it help you write your winning headline? If not, consider it for your NDL. It might look like "don't read data packs from the UX team this month as they pivot their reporting," "don't look at data about Europe launch," or "don't read study on new ventures." These may be important to someone else, but you're choosing to spend your time in a better way.

Avoiding data and information can be high risk. After all, in many jobs, you are paid to collect data and information, analyze it, and make smart decisions. What if we don't look at the right data? What if we make a poor decision because we missed something? Truth is, you might also make a poor decision because you tried to analyze the wrong things or ran out of time. Your NDL is your life raft to prevent you from drowning in the data. Try this, for the next two weeks at work, make a note of all the information and data that you consume. Then rank it on a scale from one to five as to how useful it was to making progress against your focus areas or informing decisions. The low-ranking things are targets for our NDL. These are the top sources we should consider adding to our NDL for the coming weeks and months. These are the data sources we won't spend time with. Even just thirty minutes back each week not consuming untrusted or unhelpful data would get us twenty-six hours back each year..

We're only talking about the information and data in a work setting that are wasting our precious hours and holding us back from our goals. There will be other data and information that you purely enjoy consuming. I'm sure you get personal benefit and leisure out of learning about various topics. We all do. Maybe you are naturally very curious. You should not add general learning and information that you enjoy to your NDL. Use your NDL to free up time for more of that.

STEP 14: CHOOSE BUSINESS PERFORMANCE INDICATORS TO IGNORE

Key business metrics or indicators on your dashboard allow you to track progress, catch problems, and make smarter decisions. However, greater access to data and new analytic techniques also mean leaders

THE AVERAGE ORGANIZATION COULD TRACK (EASILY) OVER 10,000 DIFFERENT METRICS.

today are inundated with more indicators and metrics to watch. The average organization could track (easily) over 10,000 different metrics related to digital, SaaS, social, sales, finance, employees, marketing, supply chain, and so on. All sliced and diced for each business, region, product, customer segment, time period, and so on. How many meetings have you been in and heard, "We may also want to track ..."? Each quarter there seem to be new additional ways to view performance and measure underlying business drivers.

Janneke van Geuns, head of insights and analytics at Google, says "The biggest misconception is the perceived need to capture and measure everything and anything. A common belief is that if you capture every type of metric, it will tell you magically what works and what doesn't. Unfortunately, that is not how we get to insights."[16]

We could spend twenty minutes, or even twenty hours here reviewing how to create a perfect dashboard. We won't. Instead, I want to make sure your time is not lost looking at unimportant metrics and chasing after the wrong business indicators. You must make the conscious choice which inputs you will and won't use to make decisions. This is important so you don't pay attention to the wrong things and send you and your whole team off to solve the wrong problems. It's like driving a car that has twenty-five new things on the instrument dashboard. Looking at them all means you're going to drive off the road. You have to be selective. The ability to look past certain metrics is hard, especially as those around you may still be trying to use them in their decision making.

You can't pay attention to everything. You can't use all indicators you have access to in order to make decisions. You must place bets. Your NDL is where you can write down a set of indicators that you will choose to overlook. Doing this will allow you to focus your time

---

16 Samantha Wood, "Google Says PR Measurement Is About Quality Over Quantity," Pr News, October 6, 2017, https://www.prnewsonline.com/google-says-pr-measurement-is-about-quality-over-quantity/.

and attention on those that matter. Select indicators that don't meet these criteria:

- Indicators that do not directly relate to key business drivers

- Indicators that are too narrow, for only one segment or region

- Indicators where data accuracy is weak

- Indicators that are not refreshed frequently enough

- Indicators that were good historically but no longer dictate future performance

As you write out your NDL, gut check your thinking with peers or leaders in the organization to make sure everyone else is not using indicators that you might place on your NDL. Commit to overlook misleading or unuseful indicators with your NDL. Focus your time on the metrics you know are important and tie to business outcomes.

STEP 15: SUSPEND USELESS REPORTS

We all have the weekly reports that get sent around and no one reads. You either are a sender or consumer of these reports. We already covered how important it is not to aimlessly consume more data and information that won't help us. Even worse would be if you were the one perpetuating useless reports around the organization.

As part of creating your NDL, look for opportunities to say no to the production of something that is yielding no benefit. Find out what reports people are actually using. If they are not using what you produce, then stop producing it. You should be obsessed with trying answer the following question: will the consumer of this report use it to make faster, better decisions? Not just, will they look at it. The only way to truly see if people are using the report you produce is to try suspending it. Stop producing the report for a month, and see who comes asking for it. When we go to make our NDL, we should add things like "stop pulling X report together" or "skip sending out the data pack this week." Your organization will be resistant to change, but you should play a leadership role in saying no. Identify where you are feeding into or perpetuating outdated or useless reports. Write these on your NDL, and hold yourself accountable for not producing them. This will give everyone time back.

Oh, your FOLLAS (fear of looking like a slacker) is kicking in? If reports that no one reads is how you stay busy in your role, you need to fix that right away. Go speak with your leadership about how you can best redeploy that time. Sitting around producing useless reports will only allow you to hide for so long.

STEP 16: ERASE YOUR "SOMEDAY" LIST

New ideas or things we want to explore pop up all the time. When they do, you think, *Yeah, I should write that down and look at it later.* Maybe you see an advertisement and make a note to check out a product. Maybe your friend tells you about this cool new show to watch. Maybe you're in a creative field and come up with a smart idea to research. Maybe you're an entrepreneur and have a unique product idea that strikes over dinner. Your team gave you a good process improvement idea. There's a cool book or paper you were going to read. There's a new dashboard you wanted to build. There is that person you wanted to grab coffee with. There's a potential collaboration session with a new team that you got invited to. There's a networking event you wanted to attend. You told a friend you'd check out their podcast. The list goes on and on. It gets longer and longer. You write all of these down. As the weeks and months go by, most people end up with a collection of these random ideas. We put these things at the end of to-do lists. You think, *Someday I'll have time for these.* Many people will even move them to a long-term list or someday list.

There's some potential value that's pulling you toward these tasks. Maybe you'll learn something. Maybe you'll meet someone important. Maybe your new process will impress people. But we rarely ever make it far enough down our to-do list to spend time on these items. And our list grows and grows. Most of these types of tasks are not central and core to what we need to get done. But we list them out anyway. We let them linger. They are things that maybe someday, somehow, with more time and energy, maybe, you'll have a chance to potentially in some way get to. We both know that you likely won't. We also know that having a list of these things floating around adds anxiety and detracts from your focus on the core things you need to accomplish. Every time you look down at this part of your to-do list, you think, *I wish I made a dent in any of these things*, or *I have to get to some of these next week.*

We need to shift our approach to this running list of cool things we want to explore. This is where the NDL comes in. We should feel good about naming the things we likely won't get to and proactively deciding not to do them. Skip the networking event. Skip the new dashboard. Skip the training that had only one interesting section. Ditch the coffee date. Don't listen to your friend's podcasts. We have to stop just deprioritizing. We can't have the "someday" tasks clinched to the bottom of our to-do lists forever. If we are honest with ourselves and know we will likely never have the time, put these items on your NDL.

Feel proud that you have proactively decided you're going to spend your time on something else. Feel proud that you're declaring your time is better used in another way. You should feel energy and warmth in the fact that you've grabbed that time back. You should get energy from the fact that you've decided to ignore the things you would have never likely gotten to anyway. You should feel a sense of freedom from these tasks. You should get a rush of motivation knowing that the things you will focus on tackling are the right things instead.

Another tactic to consider for items like this is placing them in your phone as a reminder. Set a reminder to *consider* the idea or to-do item at a specific time in the future. Use Siri or another speech-to-text feature to capture your idea. Something like, "Hey Siri, remind me on Tuesday, October 4, at 5:00 p.m. to consider revamping the sales deck with new data." Don't have the alert go off at a time that will distract you. Set it to remind you in a few weeks or months from now when you may have more time to devote to the task. Again, it's no longer floating around in your mind or at the end of a to-do list, and you feel comfortable knowing you'll be reminded again later. When the alert goes off and the reminder pops up, don't just add it to your to-do list. You need to screen the item again. Assess whether it should be just deleted or whether now it does tie to your focus areas.

Just as Marie Kondo helps you reach in the back of your closet and discard the old sweater that doesn't bring you joy, we need to do the same thing with our to-do list. We must look at the items lingering around at the bottom and delete them if they don't tie to our focus areas. Put these items on your NDL, and feel accomplished for not allocating time to them.

STEP 17: ELIMINATE, SHORTEN, OR AUTOMATE ROUTINE PROCESSES

Another one of Nike's ten founding business values reads, "Perfect results count—not a perfect process. Break the rules: fight the law." We can use our NDL to live this value too. Most organizations have hundreds of outdated processes that have been perpetuated over time. They require a substantial amount of employees' time and attention on a recurring basis. They are defined and embedded. People don't like to change them. Colleagues will tell you, "It's the way we've always done it." Many processes today were built before automation was available and when the organization was run differently. Instead of seeing our role as simply a fulfiller of a process, we need to question why we continue running processes the same way. Finding a better process and approach means we put the old outdated and inefficient ways of working on our NDL.

Declare that you will no longer spend any time running processes inefficiently. We have to stop outdated processes from stealing our time. These may not be things we can just abruptly stop, because a process would break. It's also hard to not do components of a process if you're one of many people contributing. You can't simply not supply your inputs during a given week and dust your hands clean. Things will break. You'll lose credibility. And you'll likely be coined as someone who "has a problem with process." All of which will diminish the chances of you advancing more quickly.

We're not talking about breaking a process or adding risk to the organization by just letting it crumble. Instead of just not doing, you'll have to diplomatically recommend to others involved in the process how you can shorten, skip steps, cut, or shift the approach to save time. You can also collectively assess whether the output of the process is worth running the process and potentially eliminate it entirely. We'll cover these communication techniques shortly. The point is, we need to put these inefficient ways of working down on our NDL and find sustainable solutions as quickly as possible.

The question we want to answer is, How little of your time can you allocate to routine processes and get to the same result? As you create your NDL, it's the perfect venue to question your time allocation toward routine process steps in your workflow.

While producing your NDL, stop and ask these questions about the recurring processes you contribute to:

- Does this process and the inputs still support organizational objectives?

- Can I automate any pieces of the process?

- If I had to shorten the process by 30 percent, what would I cut?

- Can I outsource any of my inputs to someone else?

- Can we run the process less frequently?

The answers to these questions will yield new things to add to your NDL. As you create your NDL, challenge yourself to find one process or routine activity each month that could be done faster or with less effort from you. Finding even one hour per week of things to not do for routine processes will yield fifty-two hours saved at the end of the year. That's more than a whole work week. Imagine if you did that every month for five years. That would compound your time savings to a potential of 790 hours. That's 39 percent of a working year.

Imagine freeing up 39 percent of your working year and reallocating it toward your focus areas.

Using the NDL to cut back the time you spend on process-related activities in your organization will return a large volume of hours back in the bank. And the truth is, leaders love those that make things more efficient. That's because most processes require inputs from multiple people. By making processes less time consuming, you're giving time back to everyone involved. Getting this right has a multiplier effect. As you go to create your NDL, find one process each month where you can challenge the status quo and gain a few hours back.

STEP 18: TIMEBOX LIMITLESS TASKS

Meetings end. Processes are complete. Projects achieve stated objectives. Travel comes to a close. But each week, most professionals also embark on some tasks that could have no time limit on their duration. These types of tasks can leave us allocating an unlimited amount of time if we let ourselves. These could be things like review competitors, analyze peer data, make materials for a conference, rehearse a presentation, do a deep dive into a client segment, launch a marketing campaign, brainstorm process breakdowns, root cause a drop in revenue. All of these are important and could tie directly to our focus areas and headline. However, these tasks could take thirty minutes or three days if we let them. What's important is to spot these limitless tasks that have no clear end point.

Try timeboxing. Timeboxing is allotting a fixed, maximum unit of time for an activity. That unit of time is called a timebox. Scrum, an Agile methodology, uses timeboxing for all of the Scrum events and as a tool for concretely defining open-ended or ambiguous tasks. The goal of timeboxing is to define and limit the amount of time dedicated to an activity. You put a box around the task and commit to spending only so much time on it. Apply a best guess for when the diminishing marginal return will kick in for certain tasks. Declare when your investment of time will no longer yield a substantial benefit.

Spot these limitless tasks in the week ahead, and add time limits to force focus and results. This will ensure your precious hours are not stripped away. You're simply declaring the amount of time you're willing to dedicate. So instead of just having "analyze peer data" on your to-do list, you should put on your NDL, "do not analyze peer data for more than ninety minutes." This forces you to allocate the appropriate amount of time to get to the results you need. Timeboxing ensures that even if you commit to spending time on something, you're not overinvesting. In other words, you're agreeing to not spend too much time on it.

TIMEBOXING ENSURES THAT EVEN IF YOU COMMIT TO SPENDING TIME ON SOMETHING, YOU'RE NOT OVERINVESTING.

If we bring the concept of timeboxing back to our personal budget for a moment, it would translate like this. Say you're at a charity auction event. In theory, there is an unlimited amount you could bid for the Napa Wine Tasting Tour. Theoretically, if we had all the money in the world, we could spend anything to win the auction. But we usually tell ourselves (or argue with our significant other about) the amount we feel comfortable spending. You enter the auction, and you agree with yourself, *I won't spend more than $500 here today.* We make a mental note of this *before* heading into these situations. Then if we spend more than $500, we feel bad about it. We feel like we went above the amount we were comfortable with. We often fail to set these limits on how we allocate our time. By timeboxing, you're making a note of how much time you'll allocate to certain upcoming tasks to make sure you don't spend too long. It's your way of not spending too much money or, in this case, time.

Put these time limits on your NDL, written as a statement: "I will not spend more than one hour on X" or "I will not spend more than twenty minutes on preparing for Y." A way to hold yourself accountable to this is to use the timer feature on your smartphone. Start the clock when you begin the task and wrap up when the timer goes off. Another easy way to do this is also to schedule the time on your calendar. If you block only an hour between other meetings to complete this task, you force trade-offs to get to results more quickly.

STEP 19: GO HEAVY ON THE DELETE KEY

Email. Yes, that tool that we will look back on in two decades and wonder, *Why did we sit there and type out long answers and wait forever for people to respond?* Yes, I'm talking about that tool. Coming up, we will cover when during the day we should turn email off. However, you do need a strategy for how to tackle your inbox eventually. It should involve your right pinky hovering over the delete key. We do not need to respond to everything we get. No response IS a response. And we should feel just as good about that. The same saying no fears creep in when we go to just delete a message. However, to focus on the important items, we have to get comfortable deleting more messages. So how do we do that?

NO RESPONSE IS A RESPONSE.

The best way is to set a delete goal for yourself each day or week using your NDL.

One strategy is to set a time limit for email. Something like "spend only thirty minutes each day and get through my whole inbox." Alternatively, you can determine upfront what percentage of emails you will delete. For example, when you sit down and look at one hundred emails in your inbox, you may say "I'm going to delete 20 percent of these." Both approaches help entice you to press the delete key more frequently and move on to the important messages more quickly. Try adding a delete goal to your NDL. This will save you several minutes (or maybe even hours) trying to write full messages back to 100 percent of the emails you received. Your spam and distro emails don't count, by the way; this is about deleting actual emails that are of low relative importance. You have to delete real messages so you can focus on hard problems for your organization.

Two other tricks. Speech-to-text works better than ever these days. Don't be afraid to dictate your emails (i.e., on your NDL put down "don't type emails" and instead speak them). I prefer to find a sunny spot outside and speak emails into my smartphone. I find that I write more authentic and honest messages that way too. Second, you can always declare inbox bankruptcy. When messages from weeks ago have built up, just delete all and start fresh. Doing so may allow you to get back on top of the things that truly matter.

STEP 20: PICK PROBLEMS YOU WON'T SOLVE

At most organizations people raise difficulties, issues, defects, concerns, inefficiencies, or challenges left and right. Regardless of level, you likely report and also hear about all these problems, day in and day out. You can't solve them all and certainly not all at once. The real problem is that most professionals will try to solve all problems and end up solving very few. In the same way you choose the battles you will lose, you should identify the problems you can live with in your organization. At least live with for now that is. We could spend chapters categorizing risks and problems and provide frameworks for how to select the ones that you need to solve versus those you can let slide. We won't dive into that here. The important step here is that you take some of the problems you could solve and proactively choose to not spend time solving them. Use your NDL as a spot to name the problem, and actively not spend time on it. For every problem you choose to spend zero time on, you can spend more on the larger, bigger, more important challenges for your organization.

STEP 21: FIND PERSONAL PERFORMANCE GAPS TO NOT CLOSE

If you're like most people, every performance review comes with three to five "opportunities" or "areas for improvement." Some may be well known to you; some may be news. Some may be simple tweaks, and others may be skills that will take years to develop. You likely don't agree with all of them. Regardless, let's assume you walk out of your review with a set of things to go work on improving. You can build, tweak, and develop only so many skills at a time. Trying to focus on closing every gap in your performance at once may leave you spinning your tires in the same spot.

Let me caveat this next section. If you have gaps in performance that are serious enough to impact your ability to do your current job effectively then stop reading. You will need to actually close those gaps, or your company will likely be showing you the door. Let's assume your gaps are more forward looking and about how to be more effective or progress in the organization. Step one is to work with your boss to classify the gaps your boss has spotted. You want to schedule an honest conversation about (1) what gaps are not allowing you to be most effective in your current role, (2) which gaps are holding you back from the next role, and (3) which gaps are more general in nature that your boss believes may hinder your growth long term. Trying to bucket your performance opportunities or gaps into these three categories will help you determine which gaps you can actively ignore. It's best to do this with your boss's help or to draft it up and get your boss's feedback.

Here is where your NDL comes into play. You must decide which of these opportunities or gaps are not worth the return on your time to solve. Or at least not worth it right now. Gaps holding you back from being effective in your current role should be the areas you do focus time and energy on improving now. These will get you the best return in your current job. These do not go on your NDL. Next, take a look at the personal performance gaps you have holding you back from the next level or role internally or that your boss has spotted for the long term. We won't go through a full career exploration exercise here, but you should be honest about what skills you may actually not need in five, ten, and fifteen years. Place the gaps that seem least important to where you're going on your NDL. It may sound like "Don't spend time learning python" or "Avoid learning content management techniques." You're not telling yourself to get worse. You're just actively declaring where you won't invest. In doing this, you shift your development-related time and attention to areas that will matter most going forward. Your NDL allows you to make this call and stop trying to get better at everything all at once. As a result, you make faster progress against closing the few gaps that matter most.

CHAPTER 10

DESIGN A DISTRACTION-LESS WEEK

I do today what people won't, so I achieve tomorrow what other people can't.

—DAYMOND JOHN, ENTREPRENEUR
AND VENTURE CAPITALIST

If you own a smartphone, you know what happens most days. Alerts are going off. Text messages are dinging. Group chats are blowing up. Your smart watch is buzzing. Slack or Microsoft Teams is popping up. People are commenting on your Instagram. If you're reading this in the future, I'm sure we'll have invented fifteen more apps or connectivity platforms that can all distract you at a moment's notice. You could literally spend your whole day reacting to these attention grabbers. Every ding and alert is distracting you from making progress toward your focus areas. Sure, you've tried deleting the apps or limiting screen time. That never really works. A month later you're often back to where you started.

According to a University of California Irvine study, on average, it takes twenty-three minutes and fifteen seconds to regain focus after even a brief distraction.[17] That's a huge cost in terms of your time and progress toward your focus areas.

Also, it's getting worse. COVID-19 leap-frogged mobile usage forward. In 2020, the average daily hours spent on mobile devices gained significantly. In the US, screen time is just above 3 hours per day, China 4.4, and India 4.8.[18] Yes, some of these hours are productive and spent on apps that help us get more done. This section is about spotting the potentially wasted time on your devices and using your NDL to proactively avoid throwing that time away.

According to Buddhist principles, these digital distractions are also known as "monkey mind," a term that refers to being unsettled and restless. We all recognize the monkey mind, when we are going in multiple directions at the same time, swinging from one branch to the next. We switch from screen to screen, from task to task. We are in search of the next banana every few minutes. It's the mind that likes to be mindless. The Mahayana teachings in both China and Japan have talked about monkey mind for more than fifteen hundred years. When the monkey mind is tamed, focused, and quiet, it has great energy and power. Chögyam Trungpa, a Tibetan Buddhist meditation master said, "We might discover the monkey is actually a gorilla—much more potent and expansive than we imagined."[19] Many people use medita-

---

17 Gloria Mark, et. al., "The Cost of Interrupted Work: More Speed and Stress," CHI '08: Proceedings of the SIGCHI Conference on Human Factors in Computing Systems, April 2008, https://www.ics.uci.edu/~gmark/chi08-mark.pdf.

18 John Koetsier, "We've Spent 1.6 Trillian Hours on Mobile So Far in 2020," Forbes, August 17, 2020, forbes.com/sites/johnkoetsier/2020/08/17/weve-spent-16-trillion-hours-on-mobile-so-far-in-2020/?sh=6ea54b6a6d61.

19 Carolyn Rose Gimian, "What is Monkey Mind?" Lion's Roar, August 24, 2016, https://www.lionsroar.com/monkey-mind/.

tion to calm a monkey mind. Using an NDL to avoid distractions helps us preserve a focused state and unleash the gorilla we all have inside.

Maura Thomas, a thought leader on attention management, shared that, "Everyone is busy all day, but they often don't make progress on the most important things," and that "The old ideas about 'time management' and multitasking are no longer working. In fact, they seem to be making things worse."[20] She trains corporate teams on how to focus their attention so that distractions don't eat away the day. These distractions are often known and recurring. Conventional wisdom tells us that if we can look at something or respond in sixty seconds, we should just quickly knock it out. This way of thinking is holding us back. Instead, we want to find all the distractions, wall them off, and ensure they don't rob our time and attention. Use your NDL to predict the distractions that could pop up and agree with yourself to look right past them.

WE WANT TO FIND ALL THE DISTRACTIONS, WALL THEM OFF, AND ENSURE THEY DON'T ROB OUR TIME AND ATTENTION.

Cal Newport also wrote extensively on the impact of distractions in his 2016 book called *Deep Work: Rules for Focused Success in a Distracted World.* Deep work is the ability to focus without distraction on a hard or demanding task that requires a large amount of brainpower. Newport reviews how deep work is like a superpower in our increasingly connected economy. He observes that most people have lost the ability to go deep, instead spending their days in a frantic blur of email and social media. To avoid distrac-

---

20   Maura Thomas, "Productivity Training for Teams," Maura: Control Your Attention, Control Your Life, accessed November 12, 2020, https://maura-thomas.com/productivity-training/productivity-training-for-teams/.

tions, he covers four "rules" for transforming your mind and habits to support deep work. Rule 1: work deeply, by scheduling breaks from focus, instead of scheduling focused time. Rule 2: embrace boredom, try not to fill every single empty space in your day. Allow your mind to wander and create for itself, rather than relying on devices. Rule 3: quit social media, instead think of social media as a tool. If spending time on Facebook, Twitter, or Instagram is a useful means to an end for either your work or personal life, then go ahead and schedule time to participate. Rule 4: drain the shallows, by squeezing the unnecessary meetings and chores out of your workweek.

It's a great read with many helpful techniques that support the use of an NDL. When you create your NDL, you must identify which distractions (in person and through technology) will interrupt our flow and hold you back from deep, focused, work on the things that matter.

A CEO-level mentor of mine at a Washington, DC–based risk advisory firm, Shvetank Shah, taught me a lesson that applies to how we can design a distraction-less day. He said when he pulls out of the parking garage each evening, he reflects on the day with a question: Was today a send day or receive day? Did I push forward and make progress toward my core objectives or was I pulled away by countless different distractions that didn't move me closer to my goals?

"Sending," he explained, "is when you sprint forward on strategically important tasks. You're helping the business get ahead by sending out answers, follow-ups, and making decisions." You're fighting off the noise to make progress on hard challenges that need your time and attention. You're on the offense. You're working on your priorities. You're calling the shots and making things happen.

"Receiving" is when distractions, questions, notifications, email, IMs, FYIs, and He always reminded me, you can't have too many receive days in a row.

Each day is up to you. Predetermine when you will be in send and receive mode across the week. Your NDL should define when the distractions are not welcome. It will define when you will not do distractions. This will, by default, isolate the chunks of time where you get deep work done or stay in send mode mode. It will define the periods where you run hard and fast to make progress at all costs, without distractions.

Your NDL is the spot where you write down and commit to periods of no distractions. You do this by putting in place "Freezes" throughout the week. Let's take a look at a few types of freezes and how to add them to your NDL.

STEP 22: FREEZE INSTANT MESSAGING

The worst distraction is instant messaging. If you've got your IM open, and your green dot is showing you're online, you're essentially waving the flag that says, "Hey everyone, my time doesn't matter, who wants to waste it … I'm right here … send me a distraction." IM can be a useful collaboration tool when applied correctly. But in this complex, fast-paced work environment, an organization can make no progress if employees are simply bothering each for answers to nonurgent issues back and forth all day long. To make progress on your focus areas, just turn it off for a while each day. Then come back and reply to people after the important things are done. Write down on your NDL when you won't have IM up and running. Pick the periods of time across the next week when you will not do IM. Even blocking a few hours each day will allow you to focus your time and attention on the things that matter to hitting your goals and objectives. To reduce the number of pings moving forward, find more scalable ways for your colleagues to get rapid answers to common questions.

STEP 23: FREEZE SOCIAL MEDIA

I'm skeptical when people say, "I'm getting off Facebook altogether" or commit to avoiding social media distractions flat out as a resolution. It never usually works, and these platforms can be useful. We don't have to be that extreme to get ahead. But social media distractions do have a time and place. On your commute. At the pool. When you're cooking dinner. When you're relaxing. These are periods when you're willing to be in receive mode. This is when you're opening the door and welcoming distractions. These periods are important for connection and social interaction. It's fun and enjoyable at certain times. But you need to define the periods that you'll let yourself get wrapped up in social media and when you won't. When you're spending time on your focus areas, freeze your social media. When you go to make your NDL, determine for the week ahead when you will freeze social media so you can stay in send mode. Write down on your NDL the hours, and on which days, you will not open social media. Be as literal as, "Don't open Twitter or Instagram between 9:00 a.m. and 2:00 p.m. on Monday, Wednesday, and Friday." For many professionals, that alone will give you at least sixty minutes of scroll time back for more important things each week. This one is hard to stick to. For more tips, I recommend Cal Newport's other book, *Digital Minimalism: Choosing a Focused Life in a Noisy World.*

STEP 24: FREEZE NEWS AND MEDIA

Do you really need to be the first person to find out breaking news via Twitter or The New York Times app? In some industries, mainly politics and investing, real-time media is the name of the game. For everyone else, it erodes our ability to focus. These alerts are almost addicting, I get it. But to design a distraction-less day, where you're running hard at your goals, define when you don't need to be the first to know about breaking news. It's okay to declare a few media freezes throughout the week. Define when you won't do news media. By no means does this mean you should not stay informed; just make the choice to do it at the right time. For example, batch your media time for breakfast, lunch, and the evening. Pick periods each week when you won't check the news. Write these down on your NDL.

STEP 25: FREEZE YOUR EMAIL

I like to call this one "shutting your virtual door." Email can be an important tool for achieving progress and is vital to being in send mode. But it's also one of the largest distractions we have. You can get pulled away quickly when you see emails popping up in the corner of your screen. A part of your NDL should list out when you will not do email. Define the times of day when you will work offline. If you use Microsoft Office, you can literally flip it to offline mode and work for a few hours.

I do email only before 9:00 a.m., from noon to 1:00 p.m., and from 5:00 p.m. to 5:30 p.m. Well, I try to stick to that I should say. It's a constant battle for sure. Ninety percent of professional roles today do not require you to be email-available every minute of the day. If you're a trader at Goldman Sachs, then sure, emails every minute are critical, but those emails are also tied directly to making deals (your focus areas). In sales or real estate? Sure, be connected so you don't miss an email from a client. Everyone else should set boundaries for when they won't use email. Write down on your NDL when you will ignore your inbox. Define when you'll shut your virtual door.

The notion of "email batching" is covered extensively in Timothy Ferriss's work, *The 4-Hour Work Week: Escape the 9-5, Live Anywhere, and Join the New Rich*. He discusses how checking email twice per day is more than enough to be successful in most roles. He has two tips that will help you automate this portion of what you won't do. First, turn off automatic send/receive and any notifications or alerts. This will allow you to refresh your inbox and check email during predetermined times when you are not in an email freeze. This makes it your choice as to when you open your virtual door.

Second, Ferriss recommends—and I've seen success with this before too—an automatic response that is permanently up. This response tells all senders when you typically will respond to your emails. An important part of this automatic response is to provide a way in which the sender can reach you if something is truly urgent. Perhaps, providing your cell phone number and asking people to text you if they need an immediate response. No one will actually text you by the way. These are two simple ways to automate this portion of your freeze. You'll feel comfortable that the world will carry on while you focus on critical work.

You'll also likely realize that many problems in your organization will be resolved without you when you wait a short while to respond. Waiting to read and respond to email will get you even more time back each week.

STEP 26: TURN YOUR PHONE OFF

I considered this step for the title of the book, because it's likely the best way to avoid distractions. Do you control your phone, or does it control you? How often do you find yourself picking up your smartphone without any real reason? Even just to see if anything has popped up, or maybe to refresh your email, check the score of a game, see how the markets are doing, or for any number of other reasons. It's become a habit for most of us today. We must decide when we will untether. We have to define when we will spend time alone without our phones. This can be the fastest way to avoid getting sucked into social media or news alerts. Your NDL can help you pick times to do this. Even just a few short no-phone blocks a week will grant you back significant amounts of time. Define for the week when you'll go on airplane mode or just shut your phone off. Put these times down on your NDL and stick to them. And don't forget to turn off other smart devices that could grab your attention, such as a smartwatch or home assistant.

STEP 27: DECLARE NO MULTITASKING TIME

Next, decide when you will and won't multitask. Many people try to work on two things at the same time, all the time. Sit in the meeting while doing email. Join the conference call while doing expenses. Meet with someone while scrolling online. We too often dial in because we're supposed to, and don't end up paying attention. Spot the important things across the week when you should not multitask. Add these time slots to your NDL. Give yourself a to-do of not multitasking during the meetings you will attend. After all, every meeting you're joining at this point should be critical to one of your focus areas, so allow yourself to fully engage.

In summary, here is what avoiding distractions may look like on your NDL:

- *No email between 1 and 4 p.m. each day this week*

- *Put phone on airplane mode, Monday to Wednesday 8 to 11 a.m.*

- *Do not read news until 11 a.m. each day this week*

- *No Twitter on Tuesday and Thursday*

- *Turn off instant messaging from 1 to 5 p.m. all week*

- *Do not look at social media before 1 p.m. any day this week*

STEP 28: ELIMINATE UNPRODUCTIVE WORRYING

How often are you working on something and out of nowhere a stressful upcoming event or decision crosses your mind? You start to get that anxious feeling. Questions start to run through your mind: *Will it go well? Will I make the right decision? What if I do the wrong thing? Maybe I should ask a friend for advice? Should I just skip the thing I'm worrying about altogether?* And on. And on. And on. We worry. We stir. We debate. We tell ourselves stories in our head. This burns our precious time away.

This type of anxiety will also strike when we're waiting for the results of something. You catch yourself running through scenarios in your mind. You wonder, *Did I get into the program? Will they pick me for that open role? Did I get promoted? Will that deal come in? Will I get a large bonus? Will I get the position I applied for?* And on. And on. And on.

Past events can also creep up and cause us to feel anxious. We dwell on what could have been better or what we could have done differently. These feelings steal our attention. We start running through scenarios in our head. What if this? What if that? Should I have done something differently? What will I do if it happens again? And on. And on. And on.

In theory, we like to assume that all our time is going toward an actual task, initiative, or process. In reality, if you're like most people, you also spend a lot of time worrying about things from the past or in the future. We've all been there, stalled because of our anxiety. It drains our time and energy. Before you know it, you've totally lost track of what you were focused on a minute ago before the anxiety struck. This will happen on and off for hours, days, weeks, and months, given the magnitude of the things we're anxious about. The mental right turn you have to take to get focused again is hard to pull off.

MAKING A FIRM COMMITMENT TO WHAT YOU WON'T WORRY ABOUT EACH WEEK IS KEY TO FREEING UP TIME AND MENTAL ENERGY.

You need a better plan ahead of each day to make sure you don't lose hours to things that might make us anxious. Now, some anxiety can also lead to progress and productivity under certain conditions. Anxiety is a fear-based natural reaction that can focus your attention on solving problems that pose a threat. When it drives you to take actions on things you can control, it's healthy. This type of anxiety can actually be productive and help you hit your goals. However, a lot of the time you spend feeling anxious is actually unproductive. When you can't control something, it eats away at you. It cripples you. You lose hours and even whole days. It does not help you make progress toward your focus areas. The clock doesn't stop, and you waste time worrying about things you can't control.

You need to pinpoint what could trigger unproductive anxiety and add these items to your NDL. Making a firm commitment to what you won't worry about each week is key to freeing up time and mental energy. Your NDL is the tool for declaring, "I will not waste time worrying about uncontrollable things." As you create your NDL take a moment to ask yourself, *What upcoming (or past) events, decisions, new pieces of information or uncertainties are liable to flare up my anxiety this week?* Don't let it get you worked up in the moment. Stay focused on creating your NDL. Whatever comes to mind, write it down.

As you think through the things that may cause worry, you'll have to decide which of them you want to proactively not worry about or not do. Again, some worry and anxiety propels us forward. You want to select things to not worry about that are a waste of your time and totally out of your control. If you can't name a sizable action step you can take to control the outcome in your favor, then, put it on your NDL. Here are examples of what you might put on your NDL: "don't worry about the comments I'll get back on my proposal," "don't worry about if I win the award," "don't spend time thinking about whether my application will be accepted," or "don't worry about if people liked my presentation last week." For past events that you still dwell on, this is especially a poor use of time. Take what you learned and move on. Don't let regret or a poor decision steal any more time.

When inevitably your anxiety flares up midweek, having these items on your NDL is a shield. It's your defense mechanism to keep your mind focused. By just naming it up front on your NDL, you will gain confidence in fending it off. Your new to do is to not worry about the uncontrollable things. When you get anxious, pause and remind yourself that you committed to not spend time worrying about that item. You may also have new things that cross your mind that you didn't expect to bring you anxiety in a given week. When this happens, we want to catch them. Write them down. Screen them. If worrying about it is an unproductive use of time, whip out your NDL and add it. Remember your NDL should be dynamic. Add additional things not to worry about as the week goes on.

Another important technique that will help you calm your anxiety is to dedicate specific time each week to actually worrying. I call these "worry slots." Block off a couple of hours a week to worry. Do this when your energy is low and toward the end of the week once you've put time and effort into accomplishing things tied to your headline. When you start to worry outside these slots, remind yourself that you committed to not do that with your NDL. The worry slots are then a free safe space to do your worrying. When anxiety flares up, you should more easily be able to get a handle on it, knowing that you have a dedicated window of time that is set aside just for worrying. The point is that you're declaring when you will and won't worry. You're not shutting your mind off from worrying about something forever. It's merely a reminder not to allocate precious hours or mental energy toward worrying when you shouldn't.

Each week, use your NDL to put down three to five things you might spend time worrying about. Set yourself up with a worry slot somewhere in your calendar, and block the time. Doing this proactively can save you at least a couple of hours each week.

LOOKING BACKWARD MAY BE THE FASTEST WAY TO SPOT THINGS FOR YOUR NDL

Still trying to find more low-value things for your NDL, try this. Track your time for a week like a consultant. Write out how you allocated every thirty-minute block of time for five business days, and review it. This includes all minutes allocated to working. There are time-tracking apps that can be easily downloaded and used to capture how you spent your time across the week.

At the end of the week, once you have a breakdown of how you spent all your time, create two lists. The first list is for those activities that got you closer to success in your focus areas. The second list is for things that did not get you closer to success in your focus areas. Put everything from the past five days into one of these two lists. Take the list of things that did not help you get closer to success in your focus areas, and use it as a tool to hunt for similar projects, meetings, or drains on your time in the week ahead. This quick look backward will be helpful for spotting the types of things you need to proactively commit to not doing and put on your NDL in the future.

I hope we have now covered enough categories to at least get you started. I'm sure you can think of even more. But I'm confident we've met the promise I made you at the beginning of finding at least twenty hours of things to not do in the coming weeks. Unfortunately, that's the easy part. You should now have a long list of things you're not going to do. Next, we need to review your list, set some accountability for not doing these things, and figure out how we're going to say no effectively several dozen times.

CHAPTER 11

DECIDE WHAT CAN NEVER GO ON YOUR NDL

You cannot deliver value unless you anchor the company's values. Values make an unsinkable ship.

—INDRA NOOYI, FORMER CEO OF PEPSICO

You should now have a long list of things you're not going to do. But putting an NDL in place can be risky. You could accidentally cut and say no to the wrong things. You want to make sure you avoid that as often as possible. You want to reduce the risks you're stepping into with this approach. Before we can start saying no, there is a set of rules we have to make sure we're not breaking. These keep us and our organization safe and ensure we win back time without taking on too much risk. The previous chapters were all about finding as many things as we could for our NDL. Here, we'll look at twenty quick rules to help drive better results with your NDL. This will ensure we don't cut the wrong things or people out of our week. These are guidelines to keep you out of trouble and in good graces with those around you. Remember that building and using your NDL is a weekly exercise.

159

You can always start with fewer things and take on more risk over time in future weeks.

RULE 1: DON'T VIOLATE YOUR CODE OF CONDUCT; KEEP YOUR ETHICS

Most important: don't let your NDL lead you to make any decisions that would violate ethics or that would put you in jeopardy of violating your code of conduct or the law. Make sure that what is on your list doesn't put you, your colleagues, or the company at risk. Freeing up an hour is not worth violating an agreement you have with your employer, being sued, violating a regulation, or breaking a law. Remember that your NDL can't be used as a defense against any of these risks. Do a quick scan of what you have on your list, and double-check to make sure nothing on it will pose a threat of this kind.

RULE 2: DON'T STALL KEY ORGANIZATIONAL INITIATIVES

We also want to make sure we don't stall big bets for our organization's growth. Our NDL is based on things that don't tie to our personal focus areas or will not help us write our headline. However, when we skip the meeting, quit the project, delete the data, or end the process, we may slow down or halt something important for the broader organization. Let's make sure we don't do that. Items on your list may not be a personal priority for you, but they could be for the leaders that employ you. If something is a major bet for your company, we shouldn't outright just not do it. We need to ensure nothing breaks and no harm is done.

We need to check our NDL, and make sure we're not slowing down any key bets for the organization. We don't want projects to collapse, investments to stall, or sales to slump just because they are not a current focus area for you personally. Do a scan of your NDL. Assess whether any of the items you're not doing are critical inputs to ongoing company-wide priorities. If they are, then we need to reallocate the work, communicate to everyone involved, and add transparency about how the work will be conducted moving forward. We can still shift our time and focus, but we can't simply just not do.

RULE 3: DON'T GIVE YOURSELF CREDIT FOR NOT DOING THINGS YOU WOULDN'T HAVE DONE ANYWAY

When they are making a standard to-do list, many people cheat by breaking things apart into multiple to-dos. Many people will also go back and write down something they just did and cross it out. I'm guilty of both of these. You feel good with more things crossed out. Doing this too often, however, erodes your list. You're giving yourself credit for doing subcomponents of larger tasks or for things you know you already did.

The same erosion can happen to your NDL. Don't give yourself credit for skipping a meeting you knew you couldn't attend anyway. Don't give yourself credit for not creating a report, when you knew you wouldn't have the tools to do it. Don't give yourself credit for avoiding someone when you knew you wouldn't see them. Don't pat yourself on the back for canceling a trip when a client cancels a meeting with you. Adding too many items to your NDL that you can't or won't do anyway defeats the purpose.

As you create your NDL, you may be tempted to think, *Well, I could have maybe spent time doing that or I may have been pulled into that meeting, I could have wasted time analyzing the data.* Don't give yourself credit for these *might have done* items. Challenge yourself to find things that you were planning to spend time on and now won't do because they are on your list.

RULE 4: DON'T GIVE YOURSELF CREDIT FOR THINGS YOU ALREADY STOPPED DOING IN PRIOR WEEKS

When it comes to recurring meetings, long-term projects, or weekly processes, you may be tempted to put the same items on your NDL week after week. After all, you're not doing the same thing next week. Don't make this exercise too easy on yourself. Make sure you don't give yourself credit for not doing things that you already skipped in prior weeks. Try to avoid patting yourself on the back for skipping the recurring meeting you've skipped six times now. Don't give yourself credit for quitting a pointless project five weeks in a row. Sure, it will make you feel good in the short-term to have a longer list of things you're not doing. Soon enough, however, your NDL will have the same twenty to thirty things on it each week. This can make your list messy and unfocused. It will make you feel like you're winning back time, when in reality you need to go find more things to not do. Once you've actually stopped doing something, don't give yourself credit week after week for not doing it. Search only for new items to add each week. Keep hunting for the next meeting to skip and the next low-value initiative you can say no to.

RULE 5: DON'T PICK HARD THINGS FOR YOUR NDL TO AVOID DOING THEM

Sometimes you'll be tempted to add the scary, risky, hard, or uncertain things to your NDL as a way to dodge them. However, the whole point of an NDL is to free up time to spend on hard things that will help you write your winning headline.

You're trying to allocate more time to the large initiatives and projects that are critical to your success. No matter how hard something is, or how badly you want to avoid doing it, that can't be the reason to put it on your NDL. Screen your list and make sure you're not putting hard things on your NDL as a way to avoid them. We will advance and grow professionally by tackling these things head on. Screen your list and ask *did I add that to my NDL just because it was hard?* If you spot these, reconsider whether it should actually be something you *will* spend time on.

> THE WHOLE POINT OF AN NDL IS TO FREE UP TIME TO SPEND ON HARD THINGS THAT WILL HELP YOU WRITE YOUR WINNING HEADLINE.

RULE 6: DON'T OVERLOOK OPPORTUNITIES FOR OTHERS

There will be things that seem like you should not do because they don't tie to your focus areas. The return on your time is not positive. But as you put these items on your NDL, you get the feeling that they are still generally good and beneficial to someone in the organization. These are not others' responsibilities like we looked at adding to your

NDL earlier. These are things within your realm of responsibility that just don't tie to your focus areas right now. Things like team collaboration sessions, a team outing, a status update, or an awards presentation. They could be talking to a reporter, responding to a request, or taking a trip to see a client. These things may tie to someone else's focus areas or have a strong return on someone else's time. We all have a vested interest in making sure our organization achieves its growth and profitability objectives. Therefore, a critical step is to take a look at your NDL and ask yourself if anything on your list for the week is still important to your organization's mission and success. If you sense that it is, consider finding someone else to do that work, attend that meeting, or finish that project. You want to find someone else who would potentially have a positive return on their time for certain items on your NDL. This could be someone else on your team, or it could be someone on the other side of the organization. Make sure you play a role in finding the right person that the task aligns to.

We could spend another few hours discussing how to delegate the right work, but for now let's stay focused on getting the NDL set up correctly. The point is, do a quick review of your NDL before it's finished to make sure someone else in the organization should not actually take the item or be in the meeting before you completely don't do it.

RULE 7: DON'T SAY NO TO PEOPLE ON YOUR PROTECTED LIST

An IM popped up last week from a senior high-performing sales leader that said, "Hey, know you hate being bothered on here, but it's important. Do you have a minute?" I responded with "All good. Yes, call you in twenty minutes ... you're on my 'bother me anytime list'!"

You need a list too. A list of people you will not put on your NDL. These people know how to get hard things done and are important for you to write your headline most weeks. We previously noted that you should not cancel meetings with your boss, high-potential direct reports, new members to your team, key customers, and/or anyone you forecast will be influential for your career down the road. Put these people on your protected list. There may be others you want to add too. As you get started with your NDL, if that feeling in your gut says, *This person is important, and I probably shouldn't jeopardize my standing with them*, then add them to the protected list of people for now. Remember, however, the longer the protected list, the less ruthless you can be with saying no. Don't try to avoid upsetting anyone at all; we just need to make sure it's not people that are strategically important for our success. Once you've been using an NDL for a few weeks, you can take more risks. Early on, it's better to lose a small amount of time and preserve critical relationships and trust.

RULE 8: NEVER SAY NO TO THE EXECUTIVE TEAM OR THE BOARD

As discussed earlier, skipping meetings with senior leaders or your direct boss is not advised. In addition to that, never put a request from the following groups on your NDL: a member of your executive management team (your CEO and their direct reports), general managers, investors, or your organization's board of directors. Don't try even your best tactics for communicating that you're not going to spend time on something for any of these groups. Instead, we should use our NDL as the way to free up time to run hard at any requests we receive from these groups.

RULE 9: DON'T DISCRIMINATE

As you create your NDL, ensure you're not shutting down meetings, appointments, tasks, or collaboration time with any one group more than another. Look out for unconscious bias in what you choose to say no to. Ensure you're not saying no more frequently to those who communicate differently or have a different personality style. Ensure you're also not saying no to a particular group, such as men, women, minorities, international or domestic staff, less tenured colleagues, or other groups. Marginalizing any specific group will hurt the way you are viewed as a leader and tarnish collective employee engagement in the organization. Do yourself a favor, screen your NDL, and assess whether you were potentially planning to inadvertently not spend time with certain groups. If you notice a trend, make sure to find a way to still spend time with these employee groups to ensure proper balance, exposure, and inclusion.

> ENSURE YOU'RE ALSO NOT SAYING NO TO A PARTICULAR GROUP, SUCH AS MEN, WOMEN, MINORITIES, INTERNATIONAL OR DOMESTIC STAFF, LESS TENURED COLLEAGUES, OR OTHER GROUPS.

RULE 10: DON'T HOARD WORK TO CLAIM MORE SCOPE OR OWNERSHIP

Trying to own everything, means you can't focus on anything. As leaders progress, they will continue to add more and more to their plate. The logic goes like this: the more they add, the larger their scope.

The larger their scope, the bigger their title. The bigger their title, the more they are paid. Leaders add more people, projects, processes, initiatives, and systems to inflate the value they bring to the organization. Many leaders believe that their next promotion is driven by how many resources or projects they have under their control. However, hoarding more resources is not the way to win. Chasing after a larger scope can actually distract from your focus areas and hinder success against key metrics. As you make your NDL, do not avoid adding things just because those things help inflate your scope of responsibilities. Don't shy away from adding things because you're trying to own as much as possible. Instead, your NDL should help you cut back on owning low-value things. You should free up the time you would have spent trying to gain total control. This will allow you to focus and make significant progress on the few areas that matter.

RULE 11: DON'T USE A DIRTY YES

Brené Brown, whose work we discussed earlier, also examines how some leaders will say yes, when they really mean no. She shared that "We avoid tough conversations, including giving honest, productive feedback. Some leaders attributed this to a lack of courage, others to a lack of skills, and, shockingly, more than half point toward the cultural norm of 'nice and polite' that's leveraged as an excuse to avoid tough conversations." Brown goes on to show that "This can increase problematic behavior, including passive-aggressive behavior, talking behind people's backs, pervasive back channel communication (or 'the meeting after the meeting'), gossip,

DON'T SAY YES, KNOWING THAT IT IS SOMETHING YOU WILL PUT ON YOUR NDL.

and the 'dirty yes' (when I say yes to your face and then no behind your back)."

Don't use a dirty yes. Don't say yes, knowing that it is something you will put on your NDL. Throughout a busy day we run from meeting to meeting and event to event, pass colleagues in the (virtual) hallway, and end up in small talk with dozens of people. As we do this, we can sometimes let our guard down. We might be tempted to make commitments on the fly that we can't or don't intend to keep. We end up committing to things we know we don't have time for or we don't think are really important.

You may (even accidentally) use a dirty yes in a few different scenarios. Most commonly it happens in a meeting. New ideas are being tossed out left and right. Your colleague says, "What if we looked at X" or "What if we move thing Y." While problem solving in the meeting, you think, *Yeah, that idea may be worthy to pursue further—it could be great for the business.* You write it down. Maybe even put a star next to it. You tell everyone in the meeting you'll investigate or test it out and provide an update. Then a week goes by. The flow of the meeting is long gone. You see the idea again and think, *I'm slammed. Why did I agree to explore this further?* Or maybe the idea doesn't seem good at all anymore. You should have never dropped the dirty yes to begin with.

This can also happen at the end of a meeting when everyone around you is writing down action steps or follow-up items. You think, *I better say I have something to follow up on or to own coming out of this meeting too.* So you commit to something logical and tell everyone you'll own the action. Again, you didn't really think it was a good use of your time, and who knows if you'll really do it. So why did you say yes at all?

This can also happen when you pass a colleague in the hallway or an instant message pops up. Someone says, "You know, I was thinking it would be great if your team could look into idea X." You are often caught off guard or multitasking and revert to "Sure, we can take a look." It could also be simpler. How many times has a colleague said, "I'll see you at the event, right?" and in order to keep the peace, we quickly say "you bet!" Meanwhile, knowing we have zero intentions of going.

We know many of these dirty yeses will turn into prime candidates for our NDL. So don't agree to them in the moment. In each of these instances, you're forced to make a game-time decision. Commit or not commit. Do not commit to owning the next step from the meeting or the idea a colleague threw your way. Most people commit to chase after the new idea or spend time on something in order to avoid conflict. They want to end the meeting, seem like they are helping, or simply avoid debating with their colleagues. Defaulting to yes in these situations can crack the foundation of your NDL. It's like someone robbing you of your time and attention in broad daylight. Don't fall for it.

First, try to spot when this will happen. Ask yourself before each meeting how it might manifest. How might a low-value next step land on your lap? Ask yourself on the way to the office each day who you might run into and whether that person is likely to ask for something or request your time. You won't be able to dodge all these questions and requests. But predict when they will happen so you can be prepared. It's all right to pause before you speak. Doing so will help you catch yourself when you might say yes, and really mean no.

If the answer is no, say no. Brown also covers in her work how important it is to not zig and zag when giving a response. If the answer is no, say no, and be clear and honest. She shares a story from a global leadership event at Costco that illuminates the need to avoid the dirty yes.

> I was sitting at a table in the front row watching their CEO, Craig Jelinek, take questions from Costco leaders. The questions were tough, and 90 percent of the time Craig's answers were tough or even tougher. I've seen a lot of CEOs take unvetted questions, and more often than not, when the questions have hard answers, the leader zigzags like there is a gator in hot pursuit. You hear a lot of nonanswers: "Great question. Let me give that some thought." "Wow, good idea. Someone write that down, and we can do some discovery." "Well, that's one way to frame the question..." But on this cold morning in Seattle, there was no zigzagging, just straight talk: "Yes, we did make that decision, and here is why." "No, we're not going this direction and here is how we got to that decision." When Craig was done, the audience leaped to their feet, clapping and cheering. I was shocked. I turned to the woman sitting next to me and said, "That was really hard. He did not give them the answers they were looking for. Why is everyone cheering?" She smiled and said, "At Costco, we clap for the truth." We love the truth because it's increasingly rare.

Give people the truth. Don't commit to owning the next step on new ideas when you know later you'll regret it. Think about your NDL in these situations. If we're not sure we'll have time for something, let's be honest and let people know. In the moment. Try phrasing your response as "I agree this idea could be good. The truth is, we have four others already in the works. At current capacity, we won't be able to spend time on the new idea right now. If we believe the new idea should be prioritized ahead of other initiatives, then let's review them all and discuss where we'd cut back on others." Another approach is to agree to revisit at a later date. This could be for a day, week, month, or quarter from now. As mentioned previously, a good technique is to take the idea and put a reminder in your phone. Create the reminder to consider something at a future time. Phrase your phone reminder as a question: "Hey, Siri, set a reminder for next Tuesday at 10:00 a.m. Should we spend time creating/exploring thing X?" Next Tuesday, when the question pops up, consider whether it's a good use of time. If it still seems like a valid idea that is tied to your focus areas and doesn't fit the criteria to go on your NDL, then consider investing your precious time into the idea.

RULE 12: DON'T PROPOSE MORE MEETINGS THAT DON'T NEED TO HAPPEN

We have become a business culture that defaults to having a meeting for just about everything. Things that can be solved via email, chat apps, or online communities are often still put into a meeting instead. If you do nothing else, don't contribute to this problem. Don't propose new meetings unless absolutely necessary, and don't default to schedule a follow-up meeting or a recurring series of meetings unless truly warranted. If you must schedule a meeting, limit the length. Not all meetings need to be thirty or sixty minutes. Default to fifteen- and forty-five-minute meetings and use an agenda that forces closure sooner. Also, remember to stack meetings back to back. This way you have a reason to conclude the meeting, and it avoids conversation drifting beyond the allotted amount of time.

If you find yourself about to schedule a new meeting, ask what other meeting you would decline or replace to make this one happen? As discussed previously, this mindset will help ensure you are always churning your meeting portfolio and spending time in even more valuable ways.

RULE 13: DON'T HAND OFF YOUR TASK, WHEN IT SHOULD HAVE BEEN PUT ON YOUR NDL

Jim Barksdale was hired as president and CEO of Netscape in 1994. Netscape's products revolutionized communications, letting businesses and people communicate faster and better. He served in this role through the company's merger with America Online, completed in 1999. One of his golden rules for winning as a team was "If you see a snake, don't call committees, don't call your buddies, don't form a team, don't get a meeting together, just kill the snake."

If something is a waste of everyone's time, don't give it to someone else on your team or elsewhere in the organization. We did mention earlier that strategically important things should be passed along to others or sent back to the correct owner to complete. Continue to do that. Just not everything. Passing off low-value things on your list to others may feel good in the short term. Long term, this will harm the organization. If you have the foresight to see that something should be killed altogether, kill it. Don't pass it off to a colleague who may not be aware enough to know they shouldn't spend time on it.

RULE 14: DON'T USE FREED-UP TIME FOR LOW-VALUE TASKS; USE IT FOR HARD THINGS

Remember that the whole point of the NDL is to gain time back so that you can focus on accelerating mission-critical work. Ensure you accelerate your career by reinvesting your time saved in just a few very important focus areas. Don't be tempted to fill your newly gained time with low-value tasks.

RULE 15: DON'T STOP LEARNING ABOUT WHAT'S WORKING AND NOT WORKING WITH YOUR NDL

Take time to reflect on what you have skipped, dodged, deleted, or avoided. Assess the impact your NDL is having on key relationships, your role at work, how engaged or unengaged you feel, and how it's impacting your performance. If you notice things that are working or not working, tweak your approach. You'll get better at using your NDL each week the more you customize it and make it fit your unique personality and style.

RULE 16: DON'T DITCH YOUR NDL WHEN YOU FEEL ANXIOUS AND OVERWHELMED

There will be days when you still look down and see a list of ten to twenty things that all seem urgent and important. There will be times when no matter how hard you fight to win your time back, you'll be staring down a seemingly insurmountable set of tasks in front of you. You'll be tempted to let your guard down and stop measuring the return on your time. You'll think, *Well screw it; I don't have time to screen these things for relevance or how they tie to my focus areas. I just need to plow my way through and work late and try to get them all done.* When your to-do list has become too full, sometimes you're tempted to flip back to do it all mode. Don't fall into this trap.

When you find yourself in I'll-just-plow-through mode, you must pause. And I know, in moments like this, pausing for even five to ten minutes can seem like a waste. But you must stop and remind yourself that the only way to win is to first select items to not do. Remember: those five to ten minutes of screening out the low-value tasks on your list will actually save you hours as you plow through your to-do list. So when this anxious feeling of a large volume of to-dos sits in front of you, stop. Force yourself to delete (or say no) to three things on your list immediately. Force yourself to find the three lowest-value items and cut them. Don't deprioritize. Don't reshuffle the order. Don't work them into your plan of attack. Actually cut several things all together. You can even make your first to-do on the list "Cut three things from my list right now." This is even more important in moments of anxiety and intense pressure.

YOUR NDL IS MOST NEEDED IN TIMES OF CRISIS. During the early months of the COVID-19 crisis, when it felt like everything was urgent and important, many professionals flipped into do it all mode. In fact, right after the world shut down, someone said to me, "I've seen this movie before; this is not a time when anyone can say the word 'no' to a request for their time or effort to help the company." This is wrong. Your NDL is most needed in times of crisis. You don't have more than 168 hours in your week, even during times of crisis. But you have significantly more demands on your time. Sure, during a crisis you might work more of those hours and your focus areas may shift. However, we must still apply these principles and start with what we won't do, attend, produce, or spend time on. When you feel panic, that's the time to grip your NDL harder, not let it go.

RULE 17: DON'T AVOID ADDING THINGS TO YOUR NDL THAT HAVE A LARGE SUNK TIME

As you go to say no, or add items to your NDL, you may think, *Well, I've already invested so much time on this project or team, maybe I'll just see it through to the end.* Or *I'm almost done, so I'll just finish it.* This is a trap. Do not let the notion of previously wasted time lead you to waste more time. As you assess things for your NDL, measure future value only. A sunk cost refers to money that has already been spent and which cannot be recovered. Sunk costs are excluded from future business decisions because the cost will remain the same regardless of the outcome of a decision. We must treat our time the same way. Just because we already wasted time, that doesn't mean we should waste more. Sunk time is irretrievable, don't let it cloud your next chance to say no.

RULE 18: DON'T ADD ITEMS FROM YOUR NDL BACK TO YOUR TO-DO LIST

Once your NDL is working well, you'll find yourself winning back several hours each week. Then several more. Then several more. Over the months and years, this time will multiply and compound. As this happens, you're going to find pockets of time where you have less on your to-do list. No useless meetings to attend. No distractions. And no one bothering you. You'll feel free. The world will feel still for a moment. But you will also feel accomplished. Incredibly low anxiety. It could be a Monday afternoon where you did such a great job setting up the week that you feel completely free. It could be Friday afternoon where you've put tons of items on your NDL and won back time across the week. Then it will strike. You'll think, *Maybe I have time to do that thing I said I wouldn't do.* You'll think, *Maybe I can actually work on the project, attend that event, sit in that meeting that I said I wasn't going to.* Please don't.

You may be tempted to add some items or meetings from your NDL back onto your actual to-do list. Avoid this at all costs. You already declared these items as low relative value. Your time is not somehow less valuable now that it's free. So why would you lower the bar for yourself? Once you've declared an item to be on your NDL, make a hard and fast rule that it doesn't come off. Don't go back and do things on your NDL just because you have more time in the moment. Avoid this even when you feel like you have nothing to do. Instead, pull out your headline and focus areas, and find something that will move you closer to success.

RULE 19: DON'T AGREE TO NEW THINGS WHEN YOU'RE FEELING TIME RICH

Similar to the previous rule, when you win back time don't just chase after the next shiny thing. A quote from the Buddha is important for this rule. He shares, "The trouble is, you think you have time." Once you've clawed back all the useless things that waste your time, you'll feel free, un-stressed, and like you have extra time to tackle something else. During this feeling free state, we too often think, *What if we chased after initiative X, stood up project Y, or started exploring new idea Z?* You may start to cook up new ways to fill your seemingly free time. Some of these thoughts, ideas, and potential initiatives that you start to brainstorm may be valuable. These pockets of free time are when we may come up with some of our brightest ideas or new ways to make progress on initiatives. You can finally see problems and solutions clearly since you're not buried under a mountain of to-dos. However, don't commit to action unless you truly have the time to make progress on these new ideas, projects, or initiatives in the days and weeks ahead. We too often get caught in a "time-trap," as I call it. We mentally agree with ourselves that the idea or project is a good use of time when we're feeling free and have cleared our schedule. Then, inevitably, we get busy and have little time yet again. This time-trap leads us to then feel behind on this new idea, project, or initiative.

Knowing that your state of feeling free can send your mind chasing after the next new idea or task is important. You need to ask yourself if the next new idea or initiative truly ties to your focus areas and has a solid return on your time. The best approach here is to write down your ideas and potential projects and wait at least a few days to revisit them again. Revisit them when you are fully loaded up with work and meetings. Then ask yourself if the idea, project, or initiative is still the most important thing to chase after. If not, then move on and don't spend time on it.

As you use your NDL, you'll get better at predicting when you'll have these large pockets of free time. To truly enjoy these, it's also a good idea to plan something you enjoy during some of this time. Maybe it's working on a side project, grabbing coffee with a colleague, going on a run. Use this time to renew yourself; don't lower the bar for where you'll spend time or commit to the next idea that comes to mind.

RULE 20: THE GOLDEN RULE: DON'T WASTE OTHERS' TIME

Help your colleagues spend more time on their focus areas, and find more joy in their life, by not wasting their time. As you schedule meetings, add people to projects, send out long emails, or plan a process, stop and ask yourself if all the people you're tempted to include need to be involved. If there are people you think might be wasting their time, either don't include them or reach out to them and ask if they want to be included. As you gain control of your time, help others gain control of their time too. You shouldn't create an NDL for anyone else, but you can limit the items others will need to consider adding to their own NDL.

These are the rules of the road. These rules will help you avoid stepping on too many toes and avoid posing risks to yourself and your organization. They will also help you find the largest volume of things to not do and not add things back to your to-do list. I'm sure I missed some. There are others I'm sure you'll develop and apply to your own situation.

You should now be ready to act like a warrior, slaying the useless events, travel, low-value requests, projects, and initiatives. Remember to start small. Even a list of three to five things is more time saved than doing nothing differently. After just a few small wins, you'll start to see the benefit. With each hour you gain back and use in a more productive way, you'll fall more in love with your NDL.

SECTION III

STICK TO YOUR NOT DOING LIST

CHAPTER 12

MAKE NOT DOING A HABIT BY CELEBRATING YOUR WINS

We need to learn the slow 'yes' and the quick 'no.'

—TOM FRIEL, FORMER CEO OF HEIDRICK & STRUGGLES

At this point you're probably excited to put your list to work. Maybe you even stopped reading a while ago and went and tried it out. It's hard to put into practice. It's even harder to stick with it. We know that the world is constantly fighting against us to spend our time on the wrong things. As we fight back, we want to ensure our NDL doesn't become a thing of the past by lunchtime on Monday each week. It needs to be an always-on tool and a consistent behavior that becomes a part of who we are. We need to form a bulletproof habit of building and using an NDL to get ahead. So how do we do that? You know yourself best and how you've built professional habits before. Here, however, we provide a four-step process to help start ingraining the mindset and habits related to using your NDL.

ACCOUNTABILITY STEP 1: CROSS THINGS OFF THAT YOU DIDN'T DO

When we cross items off a to-do list, we feel accomplished. We should generate that same feeling with our NDL. Make it a routine to actually go through and tick off or cross out the things you didn't do. Checking things off your NDL should be one of the most liberating moments in your week. I find doing it as you go helps motivate you to say no to the next low-value things lurking around the corner. Doing it at the end of the week helps you think through the week ahead and create your next NDL. Either way, this will help inspire confidence in the method and give you more energy to find the next round of NDL items.

ACCOUNTABILITY STEP 2: GIVE YOUR NDL TO SOMEONE EACH WEEK, AND ASK THEM TO HOLD YOU ACCOUNTABLE

If you're serious about making this work, this step is key. Give your NDL to someone you trust. Have them check in with you at the end of each week to make sure you didn't do the things you committed to not doing. This is a tough task because it exposes you and all your trade-offs. This has to be someone who also understands the NDL concept. You essentially have to give someone transparency into what matters and what doesn't in your professional life. If your boss understands the return on your time, they should be willing to help you with this exercise. It could also be a colleague or a loved one. And it doesn't need to be forever. Ask them to commit to a few weeks. Give them your list at the beginning of the week, and then review it with them at the end. Knowing that you'll have to report how you did will help you stick to your NDL for the week.

After a few weeks, if your mind has made the shift to always focus on what you shouldn't do, then maybe you let this type of formal accountability fade. If you're still struggling and feel like you're being sucked into low-value things, keep this accountability in place. This will ensure you don't slip and lose focus. It could even help you teach others how to put an NDL in place at the same time.

ACCOUNTABILITY STEP 3: TRACK YOUR SAVED TIME

If you've ever set a budget for yourself, you know that the true joy comes in knowing how much you saved. You aim to spend only a portion of your paycheck so you can stash away the rest. You feel good about not spending money because you know how much you're saving or investing. You need to track the same savings accomplished with your NDL to elicit the same feeling. It's helpful to capture time savings throughout the week in a format where you can see the minutes and hours you're winning back. Find somewhere to jot this down. Every time you say no, skip something, cancel something, or dodge a distraction, write down the estimated amount of time you reclaimed.

You can create a smart sheet on your phone or computer or download the one I provide at notdoinglist.com. In a spreadsheet, along the left side in column A, list upcoming days in date form for the next month. Skip the first row where you'll put headers across the top. So, for example, cell A2 = May 1, A3 = May 2, A4 = May 3, and so on. List at least thirty days. Then, along the top row, write in cell B1 = "Time Win 1," C1 = "Time Win 2," D1 = "Time Win 3," and so on. You see where this is going. You then enter the time you win back across each day. Enter the number of minutes you win back every time you don't do something on your NDL.

Here's an example from my week. On May 4, I saved twenty minutes ending a meeting early, fifteen minutes not checking Facebook, forty-five minutes avoiding a pointless conference call, and fifteen minutes dodging someone who would ask me to "look at something quickly."

	Time Win 1	Time Win 2	Time Win 3	Time Win 4	Time Win 5	Daily Time Won Back
May 4	20	15	45	15		95
May 5	30	30	90	10	20	180
May 6	10	30	45	10		95
May 7	10	30				40
May 8	45	90	10			145
				Total Hours Won Back		9.25

You can make this tracker as detailed as you want and can track the type of activity, event, or person you avoided. As you amass more data, you can also track trends by day of the week or various points in the month or quarter. This has multiple reinforcing benefits. First, you feel great when you see the volume of hours you saved. You can spot days or weeks where your NDL is breaking down and tweak your approach. You're also able to benchmark

MEASURING RESULTS IS KEY FOR REINFORCING THE NDL APPROACH AND ENSURING THAT YOU STICK WITH IT.

the average amount of time saved each day and push for larger volume of time savings. Having the data can help start a sort of self-competition, where you hunt for more hours to win back each day.

Measuring results is key for reinforcing the NDL approach and ensuring that you stick with it. Re-create this table or one similar, and track the hours you're winning back each day.

ACCOUNTABILITY STEP 4: RETURN SOME OF THE TIME YOU WIN BACK TO THINGS YOU LOVE

To make your NDL successful week after week, give yourself a reward. Your NDL will help you win back a large volume of hours, but not all those hours have to be diverted toward your professional goals. Give some of these hours back to yourself to spend on the things you love. Leave the office early and go spend extra time with your kids. Plan a two-week vacation instead of a long weekend. Join a sports team. Work out more. Join a board. Redo that section of the garden you never got around to. Whatever gives you personal joy. Doing this will help you feel more whole in your life. The time saved on your NDL should spill over to help you do more of what you love outside the office too. When you realize not only a professional benefit, but a personal one as well, it will give you energy and motivation to stay accountable to your NDL.

SIGNS THAT YOU ARE WINNING WITH YOUR NOT DOING LIST

Over time, creation and maintenance of the NDL will stop being an activity where you sit down and have to think hard about what you won't do. Instead, you'll lead your day by hunting for low-value activities to cut. You'll have a relentless focus on things that matter. You'll open your calendar and be able to spot the appointments that should be slayed right away. You'll proactively cross out the low-value activities and never think about them again. This notion of less, less, less will be your walking-around mantra. When you enter each day with an outlook of what can I skip today, you will know you're on the path to success.

Another sign that your NDL has become embedded as a behavior and mindset is when you stop celebrating all the things you crossed off your to-do list. Instead, you feel accomplished based on your impact on a small set of hard, really important things. This takes a while to get comfortable with. Your NDL is working if you celebrate less frequently but for much larger and more important things.

You've now decided what you're not going to do and have ways to hold yourself accountable. Now it's time to communicate to others why you won't be in a meeting, why you're skipping the event, why you're leaving the project team, why you won't be doing the analysis, why the marketing campaign is canceled, or why you won't be responding to email or available via instant message.

CHAPTER 13

SAY NO WHILE BUILDING TRUST AND LIFTING OTHERS UP

There are two powerful words in business: Yes and
no. And too often you don't use them.

—BRIAN NICCOL, CEO OF CHIPOTLE

Let me start with a communication train wreck to highlight where this can go wrong. A former colleague of mine, Cynthia, told me about a major project she was working on at one of the world's largest banks. Her team was mapping key compliance processes across the globe. There were five individuals all tasked with this work on a two-month deadline. They were a few days into the project, and the team was energized by the work. Out of the blue, Cynthia got a message from one of the five members of the newly formed team. It read, *I need to stop working on the process redesign project. I have other more important things coming up that need my full attention. Best of luck. Thank you, James.* Cynthia felt like she had been kicked in the shins. She thought, *Who is James, and how does he have the audacity to just quit the team without reason?* She pondered this for a good twenty minutes, thinking about what James's "other more important work" could be. Cynthia was angry and fired up. She thought, *That'll be the last time I ask James to help with something.* She had included James as an opportunity to grow his experience and exposure in the company. This stung. How demoralizing to get a message like this. From her perspective, he could not have communicated more poorly. The sour taste that James left with Cynthia is what we want to avoid. We don't want anyone to perceive us the same way Cynthia perceived James. It can be unrepairable. Don't be James. We can do better.

It's hard though. It's hard because the five fears we talked about are going to come roaring in when we think about saying no. We end up right back where we started. Again, we think, *What if I say no to the wrong thing? How can I actually tell someone no? What if the person doesn't like me as much after I say no? I won't look busy, and they'll fire me. What if saying no hurts my chances of getting promoted? Will my boss really let me say no? What if I miss something important?*

This is human psychology at work. We all want to feel included and want people to think positively about us. The last thing you want is colleagues, your boss, peers, or friends to think you're not pulling your weight. So you freeze. You think, I can't actually avoid all these things I have on my NDL. You may even try to convince yourself that, in some way or another, these events or tasks are actually valuable again. That seems easier in your head than taking the risk and saying no. It seems easier because you may not be well versed in saying no. This section will change that. With the right techniques, saying no gets a lot easier. Let's jump in.

SAY NO—WITH DECENCY

Ajay Banga, CEO of Mastercard, whom I mentioned earlier, shared an important thought on decency and keeping it front and center as a leader. When we say no, we have to lead by being decent. Here is Banga's perspective: "Most important today is your DQ, or decency quotient, meaning, are you behaving like someone others want to follow? Someone who people want to be with. Someone who people trust. Someone people want to be around… It's not enough to be smart; that's IQ. It's not enough to have a balanced way of looking at things; that's EQ. What's really important is that you bring your innate human decency. Your sense of fairness. Your sense of a level playing field."[21] This balance is tough. We tend to think that when we say no we're doing something negative. We're not. However, we do have to be decent about how we say no, so we win people over at the same time.

OVERCOMING THE MYTH THAT PEOPLE WON'T LIKE ME IF I SAY NO

We know not being liked is one of the main fears that holds people back from putting their NDL to work. When you go to communicate what you're not going to do, this fear will set in. There are two layers to this fear. First, you worry about the initial confrontation and how you'll actually say no. You play it out in your head. You think, *What if the person is rude to me? What if they snap at me? What if they beg me for the time?* You wonder, *How will I respond?* Then a second layer sets in, and you worry you may damage your relationship with that person

---

21   David Novak, "Leading with Decency - Ajay Banga, CEO of Master-card," 2021, *How Leaders Lead*, podcast, https://podcasts.apple.com/bw/podcast/leading-with-decency-ajay-banga-ceo-of-mastercard/id1223803642?i=1000488654198.

for the long run. You think *What if they talk poorly about me? Will they still rely on me next time? How will I coexist with them?*

Let's unpack this. We have to start by separating the task from the relationship. To overcome this fear of confrontation and harming our relationships, you have to distinguish between the two. You have to separate the thing you're not doing from the person who you may be letting down. You're not saying no to them as a person; you're saying no to the low-value task. Unless they are on your energy vampire list, but then you're not focused on trying to form a relationship anyway. Knowing this up front is key. It allows us to be precise about the thing we're saying no to, while still showing praise, empathy, and compassion for the person we're telling no.

> WE HAVE TO START BY SEPARATING THE TASK FROM THE RELATIONSHIP.

Let's start with some quick wins that we should all try to live by. Then we'll jump into the harder situations.

COMMUNICATION QUICK WIN #1: NEVER ACT LIKE YOU'RE DOING SOMETHING MORE IMPORTANT

The first thing to remember when telling people no, is that they care more about themselves than they care about you or your time. Okay, sure, your loved ones are an exception. But this is the reality of professional culture today. Your colleagues want to hit their goals or simply get the job done and go home. If colleagues burn some of your time, most don't actually care. No matter your title, pay, tenure, or standing, your time is not as valuable to others as you may think. Not only do your colleagues value their own time more than yours, most also believe their projects are the most important, as well. You have to realize this fact when we start communicating what you're not doing. Even if we think our time is worth more, we can't communicate like it is. To be blunt: no one really cares about your trade-offs or what else you might spend time on. People care much more about themselves, their time, and their more important work. Being aware of this is vital to mastering your communications around what you're not doing. As you frame the no, don't make it about you needing to spend time on something else that is more important. Others don't care.

COMMUNICATION QUICK WIN #2: NEVER ACTUALLY SAY *NO, NOT, CAN'T*, OR *WON'T*

No. is a complete sentence. But you should never use only that sentence. We have to say more than just "I'm not doing that," "I won't be supporting the project," or even worse "Your meeting is on my not-doing list." That will make people feel like Cynthia did when James told her no. That will make you look like a jerk. Even when you're in a hurry or under pressure, don't be brash with how you get out of a meeting, project, task, or event. You wouldn't walk into a store or restaurant and declare, "I'm not going to spend any money at your business." Please don't do that with your time either. We'll cover what you should say in a moment, but right here, right now: stop using *no, not, can't,* and *won't.*

COMMUNICATION QUICK WIN #3: SAY NO AND PRAISE OTHERS AT THE SAME TIME

There is an important lesson from Dale Carnegie, who wrote the award-winning work *How to Win Friends and Influence People.* Specifically, principle number six: make the other person feel important—and do it sincerely. He shared that "The unvarnished truth is that almost all the people you meet feel themselves superior to you in some way, and a sure way to their hearts is to let them realize in some subtle way that you recognize their importance, and recognize it sincerely." As you say no, you can't diminish what colleagues believe is important and what they pride themselves on. We will lose friends if we make other people and their projects seem unimportant. Use praise and empathy to keep your colleagues' respect, friendship, and attention. Find a way to communicate what you're not doing, while showing them you understand why they value that same thing. Illuminate why the project, meeting, or request that you're saying no to is really important for the other person. Show that you empathize with why they are spending time on it. Carnegie shared a story in his work about how important it is to make sure our communications align with others' interests. I've shared it here:

> "There is one all-important law of human conduct. If we obey that law, we shall almost never get into trouble. In fact, that law, if obeyed, will bring us countless friends and constant happiness. But the very instant we break the law, we shall get into endless trouble. The law is this: Always make the other person feel important. John Dewey, said that the desire to be important is the deepest urge in human nature; and William James said: 'The deepest principle in human nature is the craving to be appreciated.' It is this urge that differentiates us from the animals. It is this urge that has been responsible for civilization itself."
>
> —DALE CARNEGIE, *HOW TO WIN FRIENDS AND INFLUENCE PEOPLE*

I read this same passage on the stage at my high school gradua-
tion many years ago. It's vital to embrace if you want to use an NDL.
Please put in the extra effort to make people feel appreciated, involved,
included, and important every time you say no.

COMMUNICATION QUICK WIN #4: STOP USING THE WORDS *I, MY, ME, YOU*

Peter Drucker invented the concept known as management by objectives (MBOs) and has been described as "the founder of modern
management." Through his lifelong study of successful leaders, he
identified that "The leaders who work most effectively, it seems to
me, never say 'I.' And that's not because they have trained themselves
not to say 'I.' They don't think 'I.' They think 'we'; they think 'team.'
They understand their job is to make the team function. They accept
responsibility and don't sidestep it, but 'we' gets the credit. This is what
creates trust, what enables you to get the task done."

Remember, people care more about their time than they do about
your time. *I, my, me,* and *you* can be alienating when used frequently
in communications. If these words are used, the listener will often feel
less like you are working toward a shared objective. These words tend to
also leave people feeling inferior or less important. They make it appear
as though you are "above" the recipient. They make it feel like you're
not on the same team. These words make it feel like you care more
about yourself than the shared goal. Let me show you what I mean.

Imagine working on a project team and getting this email from
a colleague:

"I won't be able to join the meeting today. I had the other
dashboard project land on my lap. Can you send me the notes so I
can catch up? Also my week next week is slammed, so I may need a
little more time for any deadlines you set today."

Versus an email that reads like this:

"Understand we're working under a deadline and the meeting today is critical. Unfortunately, a dashboard project popped up on this side. Mind sending over notes after the meeting today, so we stay synced up? Also, just a heads-up that we should look at deadlines together—next week is looking a little tight on time."

Which one made you feel more like you're both on the same team, working for the same organization, and trying to accomplish shared goals? The messages say essentially the same thing, but the second message doesn't leave a sour taste in the recipient's mouth. The second message reads as if the sender and receiver are collaborating and working toward a common goal. In reality, the sender is actually saying no and winning back a lot of their time. The second message feels more collaborative because it doesn't use the alienating words of *I, my, me,* and *you.*

Here's a challenge for you. And if applied correctly, this should instantly improve your ability to communicate what you won't do without distancing yourself or upsetting others. The challenge is to stop using the word *I, my, me,* or *you* in as many communications as possible. Craft your messages and sentence structure to not use these words. Make your messages about the recipient and what they value. Pause and read the next ten emails you write and try to write them without the word *I, my, me,* or *you.* It's tough, but give it a shot. Craft your paragraphs and sentences to focus on the *we.* Make it feel like you and the recipient are working together toward a common goal. We won't always be able to avoid using these words. But when you say no, act like they are not in your vocabulary.

COMMUNICATION QUICK WIN #5: REMIND PEOPLE OF WHEN YOU SAID YES

As part of your message, remind people of the other ways that you have helped them in the past or will help them in the future. Include something like, "We've helped out the team in the past; remember Q2 with the operations review." You can also say, "Excited to partner together on the upcoming conference panel in a few weeks. Should be highly valuable for our clients!" This builds good will, and they will see that you're saying no to the activity, not them as a person.

COMMUNICATION QUICK WIN #6: NEVER LEAVE IT AT MAYBE

Maya Angelou nailed this quick win when shared, "Say 'no,' when it's 'no.' Back it up!" Never use "maybe" as an option for your input or attendance. Drop it from your vocabulary. My baseball coach growing up eliminated that word from my vocabulary in 8th grade. Responding to a question with maybe meant running laps after practice. Start every sentence you can with either yes or no. Be clear about whether you will or won't attend or complete certain tasks. The worst thing to do is leave people hanging. They may still be counting on you and be doubly let down when you eventually do say no.

COMMUNICATION QUICK WIN #7: TELL PEOPLE TO KEEP MAKING PROGRESS WITHOUT YOU

After you say no, tell people on project teams to move on without you. Don't let people think they should wait for your help or input. Encourage colleagues to keep moving. Be clear about this when you opt out of attending a meeting or if you step back from a project.

Make sure people aren't waiting for you when you have put the item on your NDL.

COMMUNICATION QUICK WIN #8: MAKE IT CLEAR YOU LOOKED FOR SOMEONE ELSE TO PLAY YOUR ROLE

Tell stakeholders if you looked for an alternative person to attend the meeting or help with the project. If you found someone and it's a good use of their time, then direct them to that person. If you did not find a replacement or alternative person to be in the meeting or help with the project, be clear about that, too. Say something like, "Know how critical this is so looked for someone else to join the initiative from over here. Everyone is just overcapacity at the moment." This will pre-answer the question they might have: Can someone else help in your spot? It also builds trust and good will that you did think of aligning someone else, instead of just saying no.

These are universal quick wins. In the next section, we'll cover tips, approaches, and examples for how to communicate what you are not doing to three different sets of colleagues. First, your boss. Second, those who do value their time. Third, those who don't value their time.

HOW TO TELL YOUR BOSS NO

When I teach the NDL concept to people, they often say, "Well, but my boss doesn't think like this," or "My boss thinks everything is important," or "My boss doesn't let me say 'no' to low-value things," or "My boss doesn't understand a limited amount of time," or "My boss isn't focused so I can't be either." Frankly, these are all excuses for not shifting your time to the most important work. We likely use these excuses because we don't understand our role and our bosses role well enough.

As we get started, know that using an NLD and telling your boss about it will drastically enhance their total image of you if done correctly. Your NDL is not something you should hide or feel dirty about using. At all. Let's see how this works.

> # YOU AND YOUR BOSS SHOULD BE SETTING EACH OTHER UP FOR MUTUAL SUCCESS.

Most societies, cultures, and traditions make it hard to speak up to authority. So, I get that we're challenging long-term norms by discussing this. Before we start to discuss tactics for communicating with your boss, we might need to take a step back and think about the role of our boss. Or what their role should be. Too often, we view our boss as someone who should guide us and give us marching orders. That is an outdated and narrow mindset. You and your boss should be setting each other up for mutual success. You should aim to guide yourself and test your priorities and ideas with your boss for feedback. You should also be passing your boss critical information to help him or her excel in their role. Part of this mutual success is attained by making sure you both spend time on the right things. The title of this section might actually be misleading. We're not telling our boss no. We're telling them there is something more valuable we should be spending time on. By saying no, you're actually trying to help your boss be more successful. You are trying to spend your time in a way that will lead to better outcomes for you, your boss, and your entire team. Instead of saying no, deliver a compelling pitch about how you want to shift your time. Then, collaborate with your boss on what should and should not get your time and attention.

First, ask yourself a fundamental question about your boss: Does your boss care about how long you work or what you accomplish? The answer to this question will inform how you communicate with them.

If your boss measures outcomes, they also likely understand time constraints, trade-offs, and the need to focus. This will make it a lot easier for you to communicate what you've chosen not to do. Remind them how saying no is actually allowing you to say yes to something else that is even more important. In fact, if they really chase only after outcomes, you may not even need to tell them what you said no to. They will assume you're making trade-offs in the background in order to drive hard toward the goals they set out. Continuously tell your boss stories about how you're reducing your time spent on low-value tasks. It should enhance their total image of you. They should see it as a leadership strength. Tell your boss about your NDL, and explain the concept. Ask them to look at your list with you some weeks and ensure you're both aligned on the trade-offs you're making. This exercise can help you both come to agreement on what your focus areas should be each week. It will help

TELL YOUR BOSS ABOUT YOUR NDL.

you both work better, smarter, and faster. As random things pop up midweek, ask your boss how the meetings, requests, or projects they are sending you tie back to your focus areas. Frame this as your desire to learn, not as a disagreement with what they sent you. Simply say, "Trying to get a sense of how this maps to our key focus areas, so we can work toward success. Can you let me know how you're thinking about it?" This dialogue allows you to frame things like, "I was going to spend that time focused on X, should I now pivot and spend time on Y?" or "I actually thought we could run after project A, because we know there will be high returns from that, and we can wait a bit before we consider your proposed project B." Remember that a healthy debate about where to focus is beneficial for you and your boss. Be open to their coaching on what you should focus on and what should go on your NDL.

If your boss values their time, also let them know how you are saving them time. This will help them trust you to say no more often. If you can independently write the memo for them or can resolve something on your own and cancel your meeting with them, do it. Then make sure they know you saved them that time. Be subtle but clear by saying something like, "Know we were supposed to meet. I went ahead and wrote the draft and sent it to you via email for comment instead. Thought that would save us both thirty minutes drafting from scratch."

The fastest way to save your boss time and explain your trade-offs is in the agenda you send them before your one-on-one meetings. Show what you're focused on running after. Highlight your focus areas and headline. Then, also include a section called, "what I'm not spending time on." Saving them time and highlighting your trade-offs will build trust. The more they trust you, the more you'll be able to say no to low-value things.

Does it sound like a fantasy world to work this well with your boss? You're thinking, my boss would not be cool with this... To be expected. First, consider if that is a misconception that you have about their expectations. No harm in floating a conversation about your NDL to confirm if that is true. If your boss truly doesn't value their time and understand the importance of making trade-offs, we may have a bigger problem. If your boss measures impact through the sheer volume of hours you're working or things you do, then we may be in a bad position. If your boss values working hard, over working smart, than alarm bells should be going off. If your boss doesn't understand time allocation toward the most important things, then it's likely time to find another role or new boss. You're learning poor behaviors. Your boss likely won't hit all their objectives, or will burn out, and you'll suffer as a result. You also won't be able to effectively communicate your trade-offs and say no to all of the low-value requests that you should. This will erode your own performance over time. What's even scarier, is that you may cast these inferior ways of working on to the people you manage now or in the future. If you would be hesitant to explain the concept of a NDL to your boss because they may not "get it," that alone says enough. Stop reading. Find a new boss.

I know that's blunt, but you can't waste your career with someone who doesn't understand this concept. You'll be in a career holding pattern where you won't make much progress toward big personal and professional milestones that matter to you. You can sit there and continue to not prioritize and likely do okay in the eyes of your current boss. They might be pleased you're running around trying to do it all. They also don't really care if you burn out. That seems like a low bar to aim for. To experience rapid growth in your career, you need to find a boss who empowers you to not do the low-value things. You need to find a boss that will allow you to focus. You need to find a boss that measures impact on a small number of superimportant things.

You might think, *I can teach my boss to act and think differently and care about the return on their time and mine.* However, this is super tough and will rarely lead to productive outcomes. There are plenty of sound managers out there who understand the scarcity of time and the need to make trade-offs. Time is better spent finding those leaders and working for them. Maybe hand your old boss this book on the way out.

EXPLAINING YOUR NDL TO COLLEAGUES WHO VALUE THEIR TIME AND THOSE WHO DON'T

When it comes to your other colleagues, remember that there are two types of people. Those who measure the return on their time and those who don't. Two buckets. Everyone falls into one or the other. We need a holistically different approach for people in each bucket. We need a different way to say no depending on the type of person we're saying no to.

We first have to figure out which of our colleagues fall into each bucket. Watch those around you at the office. Are they applying some of the concepts in this book? Are they proactive about saying no themselves to low-value tasks and requests? Do you see them being ruthless with skipping meetings, projects, and events in order to focus? Try to keep a list of who these people are. You can start to lump some of your colleagues into these two buckets by watching how they operate.

SAYING NO TO PEOPLE WHO DO VALUE THEIR TIME

The truth is, you'll find it easier to say no to those who value their time. If they are also making trade-offs and budgeting their time like money, then your saying no will seem routine. They will understand that you're making a trade-off. They will understand that you're shifting time to align with your focus areas.

When communicating with colleagues who value their time, show them how you're helping the broader organization. When you tell these people no, explain that you're allocating time to something that will help the collective organization get stronger. Them included. As often as possible, explain that you're trading off X in order to focus on Y because Y is important for the entire organization to grow and succeed. These people will realize it's a zero-sum game and time is precious. They will let you off the hook because you're raising the tide for all boats in the organization, including theirs. The key, however, as mentioned in quick win #1, is to still make them and their work feel just as important.

Here are a few examples of how this might sound. And notice we don't use *I, My, Me* or *You*.

1. Project X is going to really ramp up for the next two weeks, which is mission critical to our success this quarter. The meeting we were supposed to have today is really important, too, and the initiative has upcoming deadlines, so keep going with the team independently please.

2. Would it be possible to ask another team member to help with that? Calendar on this side is booked with things related to the launch of the new product.

3. A few things popped up this week related to the near-term new-business pipeline, so will need to bow out of project X for the rest of the month, but recognize that it is super important for next quarter, so best of luck!

4. Glad that the team is making headway on initiative X because it's so important, but a new customer is demanding our time, so please carry on this week regardless, and just reach out with the next step.

In each of these examples, you're saying no. But you're making it clear that you will spend the time on something else critical to the organization. You're also telling your colleagues that you know their project, task, or meeting is still important too. You're also doing it without using *I, my, me,* or *you.* You're being open and honest that your time is precious and you're focusing on things that are vital to collective success. They will get it. If they don't, then maybe you mistook them as someone that understands time allocation and trade-offs.

Next we'll cover the blunt tactics to use with the people we put in the other bucket of not valuing their time.

SAYING NO TO PEOPLE WHO DO NOT VALUE THEIR TIME

The people who understand the value of their time and make trade-offs to protect it are much easier to communicate with about what you won't be doing. Then there is everyone else. Everyone else who doesn't get it. You have to realize and get comfortable with the fact, that more than 70 percent of people in any organization do not think strategically about their time. They don't proactively fight to protect it. These people are not

MORE THAN 70 PERCENT OF PEOPLE IN ANY ORGANIZATION DO NOT THINK STRATEGICALLY ABOUT THEIR TIME.

ineffective; they just tend not to use their time more effectively. They don't come into the office and make trade-offs to allocate their time to the most important areas. Instead, they work until 10:00 p.m. and every weekend.

There are two types of people who don't value their time, and we need a different approach for each.

First, there are those who work extremely hard but are unfocused. Let's call these the "go-getters." They tend to work on seventeen different things at once, trying to get ahead. They tend to start significantly more projects than they ever finish. You see these individuals stand up more meetings, send more emails, and involve more stakeholders. They talk quickly. They are always in a rush. They always appear busy. They want to be a part of every team. It's hard to get on their calendar because it's usually packed. But they also don't seem focused. These individuals will continue to add more and more to their workload, without stopping to prioritize. In a lot of cases, they measure themselves on their activity, rather than on productivity or impact. They usually hit their goals but are exhausted and work eighty-hour weeks to get there.

At the other extreme, you have the opposite type of colleagues who also don't value their time. These individuals go through the motions of each day, doing what lands on their lap and going to the meetings they are sent. Let's call these the "autopilots." They are not driving more activity, but instead fulfill a narrow set of activities required to hit their objectives. They dial into the meetings only because they are supposed to. They put down time with you with no agenda, usually because they want you to do something for them. They coast. They continue to run outdated processes and approaches because it's easier than changing. The autopilots leave the office right at 5:00 p.m. because the clock told them it's time to go.

Neither group thinks about their time like money. They don't understand trade-offs. They don't see the opportunity cost of allocating time to one thing over another. They simply move through each day and week from thing to thing without much focus or planning.

For both go-getters and autopilots trying to explain time allocation and trade-offs could be like speaking a foreign language. They will likely give you a blank stare, or even worse they will resent you. Go-getters will think you're putting them down because they are doing it all. Autopilots will see you as putting them down because they are just trying to get by, and you'll appear as trying to one-up them.

There are five simple approaches for how to communicate with both go-getters and autopilots. They will hopefully keep the peace and allow you to win back time. Eventually, we'll want to make sure we're educating those in your organization about the importance of focusing their time. We'll cover that shortly. For now, try these approaches to get out of that meeting, skip the project, or delay your response.

APPROACH 1: JUST SKIP IT AND SEE WHAT HAPPENS (BEST TO USE WITH BOTH GO-GETTERS AND AUTOPILOTS)

The first approach is simple and important to consider. Do we even need to communicate that we're skipping something, avoiding emails, or won't support a project moving forward? If you decline the meeting, don't send them something, avoid them, or skip the project update, a lot of times people will just move on. Go-getters will move on to the next new shiny thing to run after, and autopilots will just retreat back to not really caring if you skipped or didn't do something. So ask yourself: *Will this person even notice if I opt out of something?* And then ask: *Will this person really care if I opt out even if they did notice?* If not, then no need to even communicate with them about the item on your NDL. Just skip it and move on. If they do notice and ask questions, try one of the next approaches.

APPROACH 2: ACT OVERWHELMED AND UNFOCUSED YOURSELF (BEST TO USE WITH GO-GETTERS)

"Just don't think we can make this meeting happen tomorrow, so much going on this week. Will reach out when time frees back up! Just so busy with the end of the quarter right now." This type of no is great for go-getters. The person on the other end is probably feeling the same way, overwhelmed, unfocused, and distracted themselves. Their to-do list has no end in sight. You're almost sympathizing with them by saying how crazy busy you are. You're speaking their language. They will likely see you as being in the same boat as them and give you the all clear to say no or skip the meeting or project. You'll likely get an email back that says, "Me too! So much to get done. Let's talk soon!"

APPROACH 3: SAY SOMETHING URGENT POPPED UP (BEST TO USE WITH GO-GETTERS)

"Something else popped up, and so can't make it. Have to focus on these last-minute deadlines now." The idea here is to say you got blindsided by another request, meeting, event, or task. It's important here to make it seem like it came out of left field and you had no idea. Also, make sure you mention that you had to do it, no matter what. Again, your go-getter audience here likely has this happen all the time. They feel like they are getting blindsided left and right because they can't focus their time and attention. So communicate along these lines too. They will be more likely to understand and sympathize with you about why you can't do whatever task or meeting is in play.

APPROACH 4: GIVE THEM SOMEONE ELSE TO WORK WITH (BEST TO USE WITH BOTH GO-GETTERS AND AUTOPILOTS)

This tactic can be dangerous. We don't want to bring other employees we work with into low-value situations. But in some cases, the person trying to get your time just needs someone else to work with for a meeting, input, or project support. You can say no by deflecting the potential time to someone else. Pick someone who actually has the time or expertise to help the person you're saying no to. You can also pick someone more junior on the team who may have more time. Try something like "It really sounds like a great project. Think Nidhan has spare capacity this month, and he has also done three similar projects, so likely could help achieve success most quickly. Mind reaching out to him to start and see if he can help? Thank you!" Again, you're communicating with someone who is unfocused and running hard at tons of scattered things. Or you're communicating with someone who just wants to get through the day. Giving them "the better" person to help will cast you in a helpful light, when in reality you're saying no.

APPROACH 5: JUST APOLOGIZE (BEST TO USE WITH AUTOPILOTS)

"I'm so sorry, I just don't think I will be able to get to this." A quick apology will go a long way. If nothing else, just say sorry and move on. Again, your NDL will put some relationships at risk. Make sure to apologize where it's needed. When you apologize, you can and should use *I*, *me*, and *my* in your communications. This will make sure they know you are at the center of the apology and it's sincere.

You can think of these approaches as cards in your hand. Play them based on the situation or even play them together when needed to say no. Remember to take stock of what does and doesn't work with your colleagues. Alter your approach based on people's reactions.

Still worried you're going to burn bridges? Truth is if someone likes and respects you, they should respect your time. They should start to understand how much your time is worth. They will trust you're allocating your time in the best way to grow the organization. Just as someone who likes you wouldn't ask you to throw money out the window, your colleagues shouldn't ask you to throw your time out the window either.

SAYING NO TO CUSTOMERS

We've covered how to tell your boss and colleagues no. Now, let's tackle the people writing your checks: the customers. Being able to tell customers yes and no is one of the hardest skills needed to run a profitable business. When you drafted your NDL, we learned about which customers to fire proactively. When we put certain customers or their requests on our NDL. It means we're hopefully more focused on the clients paying us most or that are most profitable. But what do you say to a client or client request that is on your NDL? We need tactful communications with these clients about what you're not going to do.

If we're going to fire a customer altogether, we can't tarnish a relationship. You never know who a client knows or if they will be important to you in the future. If you decide to fire your client and let their business go, be honest with them about why. Explain that your organization does not have the capacity and/or capability to meet their needs at this time. It's important that you are clear about this and don't simply ignore their requests.

INVOLVE THE CLIENT IN HELPING TO DETERMINE WHAT IS TRULY MOST IMPORTANT.

We all have had the profitable customers who want something different, faster, custom, premium, tailored, automated, and so on. You and your business can't please everyone all the time. When we spot opportunities to say no or not do something for important customers, how do we best communicate that? Use a few simple steps to ensure you maintain the client's trust while essentially saying no to their request. Make them happy while gaining time back for your focus areas. During the conversation make sure it is about the client and their goals, not about your time or NDL. Involve the client in helping to determine what is truly most important so you can allocate some time there before you start crafting your NDL.

When you speak with customers about the request on your NDL, try approaching the conversation with these steps:

1. Clarify: repeat back the request details to the customer to show you understand what they want.

2. Sympathize: reiterate to the customer that you completely understand their need and urgency.

3. Apologize: tell the customer you want to do everything you can but that there are limitations.

4. Prioritize: structure a collaborative conversation where you involve them in helping you prioritize what is important for them and in what sequence. Get them to indicate the truly must-do items.

5. Outline: explain to the customer what is and is not possible. Be honest and clear about this.

6. Explain: explain the economics of your business and why their request can't be pursued profitably.

7. Illuminate: showcase the strengths of your product or service. Highlight the things you CAN do really well for your customer.

8. Negotiate: based on their reaction and what they deem as most critical, work toward a scaled-back solution together.

BECOME A NOT DOING EDUCATOR FOR YOUR ORGANIZATION

This section has been about communicating no and moving on. That's great for the short-term and will work to free up your time from week to week. Once we start saying no to low-value things left and right, we owe it to our organizations to help others do the same. We should coach our colleagues to use an NDL themselves. Start small by asking colleagues how they spend their time to help spur their thinking.

You can use these questions with your colleagues to start the conversation:

- Do you think that meeting was a good use of time?

- Do you think that project is really going to help the organization?

- Should we use that time for something else more aligned to our objectives?

- Is that really the best use of the free hours we have this week?

- If we could just do one thing here, what would that be?

- Sounds like a lot of effort, how could we shorten this?

- What are we trading off to spend time on this?

- What would we need to not do in order to free up enough time for that?

Asking these questions repeatedly will help your colleagues wake up to the value of time. You're helping your colleagues have the lightbulb moment where they realize that they are potentially spending their time on unimportant or unproductive things.

When you notice the wheels starting to turn and people are thinking about the return on their time, then go into full-on education mode. I often start by saying something simple, again in question form, like, "Have you ever come up with a list of things to avoid or not do?" You'll get the odd looks. Then explain the challenge of everyone having more tasks and distractions with less time in the day. Then explain the benefits of winning back time to allocate to things that align with their goals and objectives.

Once you feel confident walking the walk. Then spend time with people, and teach them to follow in your footsteps. We'll continue on this theme of education in the next section.

REMINDERS FOR COMMUNICATING WHAT YOU WON'T DO

Here are a few of the key points to keep in mind as you navigate your way to hundreds of hours back this year. Remember that communicating what you won't do is the hardest and least fun part about this. However, we can do this effectively while gaining respect and keeping our friends. Remember to praise your colleagues and avoid certain words like *not* and *I* that cause conflict. Remember to show your boss your NDL and proactively engage them in determining trade-offs you need to make. Bucket your colleagues into those who value time and those who don't. You will need a fundamentally different approach for each. Never fear firing an unprofitable customer or saying no to requests that will erode value. Engage your customers, explain your limitations, and steer them to focus on things you can do well. Finally, as a leader, drive your colleagues to consider the value of their own time and what they can stop doing.

CHAPTER 14

BUILD HIGH-PERFORMING TEAMS WITH NDLs

I've never lost a game, I just ran out of time.

—MICHAEL JORDAN, BUSINESS
LEADER AND TOP NBA PLAYER

As a leader, your two most important words are yes and no. Teaching your team how and when to say no is one of the best things you can do to win as a team. Using an NDL is how you teach your team to focus their time on the hard things. Getting this right is critical to building a sustainable team, creating a healthy climate, and supporting organizational growth. Whether you manage a large team today or are destined to later in your career, there is an art to teaching others this concept.

FOUR WAYS TEAMS WIN BY USING NDLs

Once you've mastered your NDL, get everyone on your team focused with one too. Think about it as a multiplier effect. If you can get your two, four, six, eight, or ten direct reports to also adopt the same mentality, then you start to propel the organization to focus on mission-critical work. The more members of your team who are eliminating low-value requests, skipping meetings, dodging energy vampires, and shutting off social media, the faster you'll grow the team professionally and the organization at large. Organizations seek leaders who can get their team focused and keep them focused amid change and distractions. The sooner your team can do this, the sooner you will enhance your leadership profile.

> THE MORE MEMBERS OF YOUR TEAM WHO ARE ELIMINATING LOW-VALUE REQUESTS, SKIPPING MEETINGS, DODGING ENERGY VAMPIRES, AND SHUTTING OFF SOCIAL MEDIA, THE FASTER YOU'LL GROW THE TEAM PROFESSIONALLY AND THE ORGANIZATION AT LARGE.

Let's start with a story. A story about a distracted leader. I was once coaching a senior manager at a large global software company, named Nicole. Nicole had seven direct reports, who were all managers. Each of the managers had a team of six to ten individuals under them. Two of Nicole's managers were new to her organization as a result of a consolidation in the business. One was a newer manager on her team named Thomas. Nicole told me that every time she and Thomas met, his agendas we're all over the place. Thomas would bring a scattered list of random things to discuss. Thomas did not seem to have a clear understanding of what was critical versus a distraction. He was running from one fire to the next and couldn't seem to stay focused on the big things that mattered each week. He also would get bent out of shape over minor setbacks and changes that were not even related to high priority work. Everything seemed urgent and stressful to Thomas. As a result of this lack of focus, Thomas was whipsawing the team of individual engineers under him from one project to the next without a focus on what actually mattered.

I suggested to Nicole (the senior manager) that she should try asking Thomas (the newer manager), "What are you *not* doing?" We wanted to see if we could get Thomas to drop the less important projects and tasks and focus on what mattered. During one of their scattered check-ins, Nicole asked point blank, "Thomas, what are you *not* doing?" Thomas froze and gave Nicole a blank, angry stare. Thomas thought about it for a second and then blurted out, "I have all these things going on; my team is running after eight different projects at once. Clearly I'm busy beyond belief, and you want to know what I'm *not* getting done on top of it?" Nicole sat back, chuckled a bit, and said, "No, quite the opposite. I want you to proactively decide what's not important ... and then decide not to do it at all." Nicole went on to explain, "Your team will not succeed without relentless focus on the few things that must get done really well. If you're not actively deciding what you won't have them do, then they have no focus at all."

This was a career defining moment for Thomas. A large weight lifted off his shoulders. He leaned in and said "Wait, you mean I can let some of these things go and just stop the lower-value stuff proactively?" Nicole said, "Exactly!" They agreed that Thomas would come up with a list of three things he would not do (or his team would not do) during the week ahead. They agreed to write this list down and take a look at it together every Friday. Thomas agreed to send the list to Nicole, and they would check to make sure the following week that those things indeed did not get any time or attention. Thomas began to find a few hours of savings each week for him and his team. They continued to commit to not doing certain tasks, meetings, and projects each week.

After six weeks, Thomas looked back and counted more than 140 hours that his team proactively saved and redeployed to more important work. Nicole also checked in with several of Thomas's direct reports and asked them if they felt like they were more focused. One team member under Thomas said, "What happened a few weeks ago? All of a sudden, all the BS work disappeared, and now we all are hyperfocused on expanding just the one software upgrade offering this quarter." That employee went on to share with Nicole that they were loving their job more than ever and felt like they were making significant progress for customers on a few things that really mattered. That was music to Nicole's ears. Thomas had flipped the mental switch. He was now hyperfocused on defining what he and the team would not do so that they could spend time on the important things.

We owe it to our teams and our organizations to help as many people as possible to make the same leap Thomas did. Teaching each manager and individual contributor on your team how to build and use an NDL can lead to extraordinary focus on the things that matter. And employees will be more engaged and do better work for your customers. To start, let's quantify the benefits of getting this right across your team. This is the business case for teaching your staff this approach right away. You'll see that it's well worth the investment.

BENEFIT 1: GROW YOUR TEAM BY 12.5 PERCENT WITHOUT INCREASING COSTS

Let's assume you have a team of eight. Let's also assume that you and each of the team members are finding five hours of things to put on the NDL each week. That's one hour per day. That means your team could be reallocating upward of 45 hours a week. That's 180 hours a month or 2,160 hours each year. Wait, 2,000 hours? That's how many hours an individual works per year in a full-time role. So gaining 2,160 hours back is like having another full-time employee join your team. At no cost. Teaching everyone on a team of eight to find one hour of things for their NDL each day would turn the eight-person team into essentially nine people. From an organizational perspective, growing each team of eight into a team of nine means we're adding 12.5 percent more capacity to the system. How happy would investors be if they knew you were getting 12.5 percent more out of each team, while holding pay and other costs constant?

BENEFIT 2: BETTER TEAM PERFORMANCE THROUGH INCREASED ENGAGEMENT

There is also an immeasurable impact from helping your team focus on just a few large bets and clearing out the low-return projects, meetings, and tasks. When a team is focused, a team is engaged. When a team is engaged, they produce amazing results. Their energy will be stronger. Their ideas will be better. Their impact will be faster. And we'll retain these employees longer. Teaching employees the importance of their time and helping them to

WHEN A TEAM IS FOCUSED, A TEAM IS ENGAGED. WHEN A TEAM IS ENGAGED, THEY PRODUCE AMAZING RESULTS.

build a mental muscle for better time allocation will lead to a new sense of autonomy. They will value their work, knowing that you're not wasting their time and effort. Teaching employees to spot things to not do, and then supporting them in not doing those things, will also enhance their feelings of ownership.

BENEFIT 3: HEALTHIER WORKPLACE CLIMATE

Too many leaders in the workplace today allow their team to waste time, only partially leverage what they produce, or let people stray from organizational priorities. When you're on a team and see this happening, it can sap your energy. Being on a team where you know this is not happening is a morale boost for everyone. We want our teams to know that what they are focused on has been screened and vetted and aligns with critical priorities for the organization. Your team's climate will become more positive when team members know they are focused on what matters. Teams that believe that their manager is thinking about the individual return on their time will have a greater amount of trust. A team with more trust means better work is produced.

BENEFIT 4: YOU WILL BE SEEN AS A STRONGER LEADER

If your team knows you're actively helping them to reallocate their time to be more successful, they will love it and love you. If done well and done consistently, your team will talk it up. They will mention it to other managers and your boss. They will provide comments in your review such as, "My manager is always making sure we're focused on our goals" or "My manager makes sure what we work on is meaningful and impactful to clients" or "My manager gets a lot of the useless and unproductive work out of my way" or "My manager is great at helping me make trade-offs and avoid low-value work." All of these are hallmarks of a great leader and things your boss and other leaders will enjoy hearing about. They will see you as a more strategic leader. This will translate into more near-term rewards and open doors for larger leadership opportunities more quickly. Teaching your team what not to do will help you advance your career more rapidly.

TEACH YOUR TEAM HOW TO BUILD AND DEPLOY NDLs

We learned earlier that having clear focus areas is a vital step to building your own NDL. Your team must also have clear focus areas to get started on their NDLs. Without clear focus areas your team could be saying no to all the wrong things. You owe it to your team to continuously clarify the few things that matter. As a leader, you should be setting the focus areas. Share these focus areas three times more often than you think you should. Bring these focus areas up again and again until the team can recite them clearly. Alter these focus areas as infrequently as possible. As we teach staff how to build their NDL, ensure they use these focus areas as the way to focus their time. They should look for things to skip, dodge, and delete that don't tie to the focus areas. When staff share their NDLs with you, make sure that the things they are saying no to do not harm progress toward these focus areas. Try an exercise to see if your team is ready to jump into using NDLs.

Ask each member of your team to write down what they believe the focus areas are for your team. Make sure to include all staff in your reporting line. Ask someone to collect what your team sends in and make their submissions anonymous. You want to ensure people give you an honest answer. Compile the anonymized results, and see how aligned your team is with focus areas you believe are most important. You want to assess whether or not the majority of your team knows and can articulate what is mission critical. They may have focus areas worded slightly differently or in a different order. That's okay. You want to make sure that at least 90 percent of your team is aligned on what is truly important. When you get the list back from staff, look for two things:

- Are team members able to consolidate their list of focus areas down to just a few items? Or are they simply listing out everything they are working on?

- Assess whether team members are listing out focus areas that are actually not important. Are they potentially including things that feel random or are old priorities your team had in the past?

By reviewing these two elements, you'll be able to see how well your staff understand and have internalized the focus areas that you have set out as a leader. Keep in mind that not all staff are good at listing, remembering, or clarifying. Don't make any assumptions about how well your team is aligned to the focus area based on a few outliers. Some team members may just need more hand holding and coaching about what matters most.

Another way to run this exercise is by creating a quick online survey (use a Google form and hide the participant names). Include your team's focus areas, but mix them in alongside a random list of other tasks, projects, and priorities. Ask staff to select or rank the things that matter most. The results will quickly tell you how well your team is aligned to the focus areas. Did they select the true focus areas, or did the results come in all over the place?

If you find that staff lack clarity on what the focus areas are, then you need to fix that first before you can teach them how to build an NDL. If this is the case, then you're overdue to pull your team together and clearly state your team's focus areas. We need to make sure everyone is rallying around the right things. This is a vital exercise and step to make sure our team sets sail on the right path with their NDLs.

Now, let's assume priorities are clear. How do you teach your team to create the list? This section will teach you how to get your team bought into the NDL concept and use it on their own.

> ## WE NEED TO MAKE SURE EVERYONE IS RALLYING AROUND THE RIGHT THINGS.

START BY TEACHING STAFF WHO ARE LEAST FOCUSED AND WASTE THE MOST TIME

Before you broadly roll out the NDL framework, decide whether everyone on the team needs to adopt it all at once. Everyone can benefit from an NDL. But if your team is operating well and achieving success, you may want to roll this out to select staff at the start. Try this exercise to pinpoint who on your team will benefit most from using an NDL. Take a list of everyone on your team and ask the following questions about each person. If you can answer yes to any of these questions about a team member, prioritize helping them build an NDL sooner than others.

- Does this team member try to work more hours than others on the team?

- Does this team member seem unexpectedly overwhelmed by their current workload?

- Does this team member measure the quantity of what they produce instead of impact?

- Does this team member volunteer for every opportunity?

- Does this team member work on things that are not a priority?

To be clear; these are not poor qualities or less desirable characteristics on face value. All teams, even successful ones, have staff in these groups. They only help us pinpoint which staff may have trouble saying no. They are leading indicators that tell us which staff may have the most to gain from using an NDL. These staff may also struggle more to apply an NDL to their workflow. Use the results of this exercise to pinpoint who you may need to spend more time with as you roll this out. If you take a blanket approach to rolling out the NDL across your full team, your strong performers who use their time well, could feel marginalized. They may have fewer hours to win back right away. Start where you will see the highest return from getting people on your team focused.

Keep in mind that not all staff will be able to flip their mindset and use an NDL. We should give everyone a shot and get as many staff using an NDL as possible. At the end of the day, it's a leadership competency that may be too difficult for some members of your team to ever grasp.

As you teach these groups about an NDL, your explanation of the benefits will need to vary. For example, those who are achieving success, but working too many hours, should see their NDL as a way to calm their life down. Those who can't focus need an NDL as a performance management tool to make sure they hit their goals. Each team member will have unique needs for an NDL. You can conduct a team-wide training on NDLs, but you'll need to teach each staff how and why to use their NDL one-on-one. Next, we'll review techniques to ensure we roll this out in a way that is self-sustaining for all staff.

TEACH STAFF THE BENEFITS AND ASK THEM TO CREATE THEIR NDL

We already showed how the NDL will get you countless hours back, help you achieve your goals, and ensure you devote more time to the things you love. Reference that section as needed when convincing your team to build their first NDL. Explain the business case personally and professionally for them. Outline how it will help them live a more balanced life and get ahead more quickly. After you've taught your team what an NDL is and the benefits of applying it, task them with making one. Remember to start small. Even finding a few hours a week of things to say no to can yield a large volume of time that can be reinvested. You'll have to slow down and remember how hard it was for you to say no the first twenty times. Sympathize with them and watch their behavior carefully. Make sure they know that the fears of saying no are natural and that you support them.

TEACH YOUR EMPLOYEES TO HUNT; DON'T DICTATE YOUR EMPLOYEES' NDLs

It can be tempting to just tell our staff what to not do each week. This will work for a few weeks but can cause disengagement in the team and won't teach them how to build their own NDL. Giving your staff their NDL will not have the same effect. We want staff to build this muscle on their own. Building the NDL themselves is where staff learn to assess the value of everything they spend time on across the week. We want staff to get in the habit of screening every request for their time against their focus areas.

The goal is for them to bring you their NDL and be excited that they found so many things to say no to each week. Remember, as a leader, to stop and listen when your staff brings you a list of what they want to say no to. It might not be the same things you would say no to. Hear them out. It's a vital learning opportunity in which you can absorb critical insight about your business and the trade-offs your staff want to make.

> BUILDING THE NDL THEMSELVES IS WHERE STAFF LEARN TO ASSESS THE VALUE OF EVERYTHING THEY SPEND TIME ON ACROSS THE WEEK.

Once you get the NDL concept up and running on your team, you can suggest things that staff should consider for their NDL. You can help guide them to spot the things they should say no to. During your one-on-ones, it can be helpful to make suggestions. Always phrase it as a question: "Is this maybe something you want to consider for your NDL?" or "What else could you spend this time on?" or "Does that help us make progress toward our goals?" You're giving them a hint that the activity, event, meeting, etc. in question should maybe be on their NDL. But when phrased as a question, you're still helping develop the mental muscle of screening all activities for the value of their time. You're teaching them to ask important questions about their time independently. We hope they start running through these questions in their head at the start of each day and as they plan their weeks.

HOLD STAFF ACCOUNTABLE FOR BUILDING AN NDL

Set the expectation that they share their NDL with you each Friday for the week ahead. It's important to add this accountability for at least the first several months. Ensure they know you're doing this to help them win back time, not micromanage them. Remind them that you're helping them find more things not to do, not giving them more work. As they learn to build and use their NDL, it's okay to relax this expectation. To help make it more routine, you can send a recurring fifteen-minute calendar block (marked as free) every Friday afternoon. This will remind staff to send you their NDL for the week ahead. Build a rhythm of collection that works for you and your staff.

PRESSURE-TEST STAFF NDLs

As you're starting this journey with staff, block time to review their NDLs with them. They will be looking to you to pressure-test why certain items are on their NDL. Go through each item on their NDL and see if you think any of them are too risky for the individual or your organization. If you were in their shoes, would you make the same trade-off to not do the item in question? Use the following questions to help guide a discussion with staff and help them arrive at the right decisions semi-independently.

- Does this task, meeting, or initiative tie back to your annual objectives or focus areas?

- What's at risk if you don't do this?

- How will you communicate this?

- Are we avoiding something hard by not doing this?

- Would we as a team never get to this thing anyway?

- Why are you dodging this person?

- Is this someone else's job, and should we give it to them?

- What will happen if you skip the meeting?

- Are there other people better suited to run that initiative or task?

- What will you be able to do with this hour instead?

- How should we redeploy this time to accomplish your goals?

Some of their responses will spark a conversation in which you can offer coaching about what trade-offs you think they should make. After they come to you with their list, it's fine to offer your advice about what should or should not be on their NDL for a given week. This type of instruction is okay at this juncture, because staff have at least produced the initial list on their own. They went out and hunted for the first round of things to put on their NDL. That's a win.

PUSH STAFF TO FIND AT LEAST ONE MORE THING EACH WEEK FOR THEIR NDL

As staff create their NDLs, they will find the first layer of things to skip and say no to. But we don't want them to stop there. It's our job as leaders to push staff to make sure they find more things to not do each week. It's on us to push the envelope further to ensure they are truly winning back as much time as possible for the things that matter. A few weeks into using an NDL, staff may start to feel stuck. Challenge them to find one more (new) thing to skip or not do each week that would have otherwise eaten away their time.

WHEN YOU ALLOCATE NEW WORK, ASK STAFF WHAT THEY CAN STOP DOING FIRST

When the next project, request, or initiative pops up, pause. Do not package it up and delegate it. If you believe it's important for them to work on, you need to make room for it. First, ask your staff, "If I needed five hours of your time, what would you stop doing to gain five hours back next week?" Engage in a dialogue with them about what the lowest-value things are that they can stop doing. Once you have agreed to what they can stop spending time on, have them add those things to their NDL. Now, you have sustainably created space for that staff member to excel at the new project, request, or initiative. Without this step, the employee may try to do it all and burn out. Or worse, they may try to do it all and fail on multiple fronts. They may also trade-off the wrong thing to free up time and get to a subpar result on another aspect of their work. Have the conversation with them about what goes on their NDL in advance of allocating new work.

DON'T TREAT ALL TEAM MEMBERS EQUALLY

Some staff will get the hang of the NDL overnight, and others may never flip the switch. As a leader, figure out who on your team will need more coaching. Spend time supporting staff members who don't get the hang of it right away. Collaborate with them the same way you would want your boss to help you find the right places to say no. Other staff, who get the hang of it quickly, don't need your time or attention. In fact, ask the team members who get the hang of it to lean in and encourage others on the team to take more risk. You can have them aid in pressure-testing other staff's NDLs. You can also have them share their NDLs as examples and talk about how they created it. There will also inevitably be staff that lose focus easily or revert back to wasting time on low-value requests. Spot these individuals and spend more time with them. Make sure staff don't try it for a few weeks and then slip back into their prior ways.

HOLD STAFF ACCOUNTABLE: MAKE SURE THEY DIDN'T DO

Make sure things don't slip midweek. Ping your team, and make sure they are sticking to their list. One approach for accountability is to ask them to send you their completed NDL at the end of the week and cross off the things they truly didn't do. Another, potentially more powerful one, is to ask them to describe how they feel at the end of the week. Did they get run over with pointless requests, meetings, and low-value initiatives? Or did they (hopefully) feel empowered to own their precious time and allocate it to only high-value things? Having a conversation about outcomes and how they felt may be more motivating to some employees than simply running through a list of stuff they avoided.

SPEND TIME PRACTICING COMMUNICATION WITH YOUR TEAM

Your team is going to screw up how they deploy the NDL and how they say no. Be ready. I bet you get cc'd into an email in the first week where one of your staff says to a colleague, essentially "Well, this is on my NDL, so I can't help you." Try to get ahead of that. Stress the communication techniques outlined previously. Overinvest in practicing with staff or editing their email and IM responses to start. We can't let them get the communications piece wrong. It could look bad for you if they don't communicate well or use the wrong tone and approach.

Teach the team that what they share with you about why items are on their NDL each week is not what they should share with others in the organization. As your staff start to identify and put things down on their NDL, ask them this question for each item: How do you plan to communicate that you're not doing that? The best coaching here will start with questions, rather than answers. Many times staff will have a totally viable plan and a way to communicate that makes sense and will not put them or you at risk. If they don't, pause and help them craft their approach to getting out of the task or meeting at hand. Practice with them. Run through a mock scenario and assess how they will communicate. Helping staff craft their communications about why they are not doing something will build trust.

ALWAYS HAVE YOUR TEAM'S BACK

Ensure that once you and your team members commit to not do something, you back each other up. Here are a few things to be on the lookout for to ensure a supportive environment.

First, try to never renege on a task, meeting, or project you told a team member they could put on their NDL. If you and your staff agree that something goes on their NDL, try your best never to move that thing back onto their to-do list or ask them why it didn't get done. Even doing this just a couple of times as a manager (even by accident) will break down the trust your employees are putting in you and this approach.

IF YOU AND YOUR STAFF AGREE THAT SOMETHING GOES ON THEIR NDL, TRY YOUR BEST NEVER TO MOVE THAT THING BACK ONTO THEIR TO-DO LIST OR ASK THEM WHY IT DIDN'T GET DONE.

Second, make sure your whole team commits to the same projects and meetings on their NDLs. If you allow one staff member to add something to their NDL, make sure everyone adds it. Don't play favorites. You'll burn trust on the team if one team member sees another not doing something that you're still making everyone else do. Exceptions exist of course, but try to be equitable in what staff can add to their NDL.

Third, defend your team. If staff skip something you agreed they should, ramp off a less critical project, or avoid an energy vampire, stand up for them. When another colleague comes to you and says, "One of your staff said they can't attend or support this project," have their back and stand up for them. Always defend them. You will destroy trust immediately if you come down on your team members when this happens. Your team member may need more coaching on the correct communication techniques. But if you both agree something can go on their NDL, then it stays on their NDL. It's our duty to defend their NDL and support them in navigating these tough trade-offs.

DON'T ALLOCATE THINGS THAT SHOULD BE ON STAFF NDLs

Once you have your team using NDLs, don't send them tasks, meetings, or projects that should be on their NDL. Screen these things out for them. Remember the rule we covered earlier; never put direct asks or tasks from your boss on your NDL? Well, your staff are thinking the same thing. When you directly ask them to own something, they will just own it and not screen it for their NDL. So be careful what you delegate. As managers, we may accidentally delegate something that is not important for anyone to actually be doing. Try to spot those tasks and put them on your own NDL as opposed to sending them down the chain. If it's something no one on your team should spend time on, then as a leader, eliminate the task, project, or meeting proactively for your team.

TELL YOUR TEAM WHAT YOU DIDN'T GIVE THEM

When you do proactively say no to something on behalf of your team, tell them you did. For example, if another leader asked your team to support something, and you said no, get credit for that! Let the team know that you're looking out for projects, tasks, and initiatives to cut on their behalf. Also, quantify the time that you gifted them back. Tell them, "We could have spent twelve hours on this additional project, but I wanted to give everyone time back next week." This will build a lot of trust. Also, explain why you placed the item on your team's collective NDL, and the logic you used. These examples will help them build their NDL muscle. Say something like, "We could have spent seven hours of the next week in meetings, but I'd rather have you invest that time back into initiative X. That's because initiative X better aligns with our current mission this quarter because of Y." Make sure they see how much time you saved them and where they should allocate that time instead.

SET NOT DOING OBJECTIVES FOR YOUR TEAM

When you can clearly see that something is draining time for multiple people on the team, call it out. This might be a meeting, initiative, metric, process, or distraction that is broadly impacting your team. Be clear with the entire team and say universally "We all should not spend any time on that." Be direct and clear when you see opportunities for your team holistically to redirect their time. This doesn't mean you're creating their collective NDL. You're simply helping them see potential drains on everyone's time and quickly course correct. Thank them for their intent of trying to chase after whatever the thing was. But then, use the words *we all* and *not* together. "We all should not spend any time on that." Show them that you, them, and their colleagues, will not be allocating any of "our" precious hours toward that thing. Give the all clear for everyone on the team to put it on their NDL.

This can also expand into strategy or objective setting conversations with your team. You can use this same concept of an NDL as a strategy tool. As a leader, part of setting a sound and focused strategy is defining where you won't put resources or focus efforts. Remember the quote we referenced earlier from Michael Porter, "The essence of strategy is choosing what not to do." The NDL can be used as a way to keep your team focused across the year by clarifying where they should not spend any time or effort.

To really make this stick, we can take it even one step further. In your team's annual objectives that are cascaded through your organization, add some qualitative not doing objectives. This will help flip the team's mindset to feel rewarded for avoiding low-value work. Imagine if you wrote into your team's objectives, things like, "Do not update the market dashboard each month," "Do not spend time with customers who are in a certain segment." "Do not attend conferences without a clear tie to our work," "Do not fulfill requests for the ad-agency team until the end of each month," "Avoid any meeting with the production team in Q1." If everyone on the team has the same not doing objectives, they have a head start on items to add to their NDL each week. Not doing objectives helps everyone work collectively on more of the right things and keeps the whole team focused.

KEEP COMMUNICATIONS AND MEETINGS SHORT AND TO THE POINT

To help your team focus, keep recurring meetings to a minimum, limit meeting length, always use an agenda, and get to the main points quickly. If your team wants to collaborate and spend more time together to build community or execute a project, that's great. But from a top-down perspective, you should give your team as much freedom to deploy their hours in the best way possible.

USE A NOT DISCUSSING LIST IN CERTAIN MEETINGS

We've all walked out of meetings and thought, "wow, so-and-so really derailed what we were trying to accomplish" or "can't believe we spent half the meeting talking about XYZ." We need fewer meetings like that. Your NDL can help. Decide what you will not discuss before the meeting starts. Provide a list of what the team should avoid digging into. This will help your team drive the right conversations, frame the right problems, and target solutions.

This concept is similar to a "parking lot" for ideas during a meeting. However, a "not discussing list" clarifies in advance what you and your team won't burn time talking about in the meeting. Of course, we don't want to squander risks or opportunities or diminish staff engagement. But if you know your team may get off track, lose focus, or go down a rabbit hole, then let's help them.

Put an NDL out there for the meeting as part of the broader agenda. Clarify that this meeting is not the place to get lost or go off topic. Name the off-limit topics up front. Then, open a shared note during the meeting. If off-limit topics come up, ask team members to jot down their thoughts on the shared note. This will make everyone feel heard. Commit to them that you all will look at those items at a later date and in another setting. This keeps the flow of the meeting centered on the important challenges you're trying to solve. This will help you and the team use precious meeting time most effectively and run fast toward solving harder problems.

HELP YOUR STAFF WRITE A LEADERSHIP USER MANUAL

Adam Bryant, the "Corner Office" columnist for the *New York Times*, posed a provocative question with the title of his 2014 article: "What If You Had to Write a 'User Manual' About Your Leadership Style?" In his article, Bryant describes how transparency about our work style—our preferences, values, quirks, and all—shortens the learning curve for others by making explicit things that might otherwise take months, or even years, to uncover.[22] Practically, this looks like a one-page document that provides instructions about how best to work with you. It covers how you prefer to communicate (e.g., I use IM only a few times a day), your strengths and weaknesses (e.g., I will always ask for help with CRM systems; I can help pressure-test marketing materials), and how you make decisions (e.g., I'm analytical and always need more data).

As I studied what leaders listed on their user manuals, it struck me: What a perfect place to also describe how you value time and where you will and won't spend it. To help your team better understand your NDL, create your own leadership user manual. Then encourage

---

22   Adam Bryant, "What If You Had to Write a 'User Manual' About Your Leadership Style?" LinkedIn, January 6, 2014, https://www.linkedin.com/pulse/20140106124338-35894743-what-if-you-had-to-write-a-user-manual-about-your-leadership-style/.

your staff to do the same. You should declare the types of meetings, events, travel, data, and projects that you will and won't do. You should also be clear about time-saving practices that you value (e.g., sending decks twenty-four hours in advance, using agendas for every meeting, never just showing data without insights). Have your staff build something similar and declare the core philosophies behind their NDL. Leadership user manuals for you and your staff will add transparency for everyone in the organization.

As staff build their manuals, set up a time to all share and discuss them as a team. Allow staff to ask each other questions about what they put down regarding their philosophies on time and prioritization. Allowing staff to document and share a leadership manual with this information will help them say no to low-value tasks, requests, projects, and distractions more easily. Staff can lean on their manual as a way to gain confidence in saying no more frequently.

TELL YOUR TEAM THE THINGS YOU STILL WANT TO SEE AND HEAR ABOUT; OTHERWISE THEY MAY THINK YOU DON'T HAVE TIME FOR ANYTHING

There is one huge risk as a manager with taking the NDL too seriously. Your team will learn how much you value your time. As such, they may be reluctant to bring you critical feedback, information, problems, or data. Imagine hearing about a significant business risk three weeks after you could have mitigated it. Then imagine asking your team why they hesitated about alerting you earlier and your team saying, "I know how focused you are on spending your time on the important things, and I wasn't sure if this was important." You would feel awful. Don't be so blunt that your team is afraid to send you things. Always remind your team that sharing information is important. To save time, make it clear that you expect synthesis, context, highlighted risks, insight, or conclusions to what they bring to you. You can determine where you want to dig in further and allocate time to what they send you. Always say thank you and encourage them to come forward with information, concerns, and ideas. Give staff examples of things that are definitely not a waste of your time. Also, highlight team members who continue to speak up and share critical information even when you are both using an NDL. This is vital to make sure we don't choke off information flow from the front line. If they think you never have time, they will sit silent. Sitting silent can harm the business.

USE THE NDL AS A LITMUS TEST FOR ADVANCING

Focusing is hard. Saying no is hard. We should look for these leadership skills in the employees we reward and promote. We should reward the behaviors related to making trade-offs that allow someone to make significant progress in key areas. It's not the main criteria to use, but it's worth a discussion when reviewing our team. Ask, does this employee say no to low-value activities and meetings frequently? Do they think about their time strategically and allocate it to the areas of greatest return? Or conversely, Does this employee run around and try to do

> FOCUSING IS HARD. SAYING NO IS HARD. WE SHOULD LOOK FOR THESE LEADERSHIP SKILLS IN THE EMPLOYEES WE REWARD AND PROMOTE.

everything? Are they scattered and unfocused? We know we must focus to win individually and as a team. Reward employees who have the ability to do this well.

DO NOT PROMOTE THE DO-IT-ALL EMPLOYEE

Being chronically busy has become a badge of honor at too many companies today. The busier you are, the more important you are. However, according to Tim Ferriss, "Being busy is a form of laziness—lazy thinking and indiscriminate action." Make sure as you reward and promote people, you don't confuse activity and output (sheer number of things produced) with quality and impact on the organization. Make sure the rest of the team knows promotions are granted because that person did a few really important things very well that helped them accomplish their objectives. Frank Blake, former Home Depot CEO, who turned the company around from 2007 to 2014, articulated this point well. During a 2020 interview with David Novak, former CEO of Yum! Brands, Blake shared, "Pay attention to what you recognize and celebrate in your organization, because that is what you're going to get. How clear is their CEO in what he or she actually wants? The clearest way to communicate is through what you recognize and celebrate."[23]

The takeaway for you is celebrate focus. If you promote someone based on activity and output, you could create a very unfocused team. If your team thinks, *Wow, if I just run around until I burn out and try to "do it all" I'll get promoted too,* that will erode focus on your team. If that mentality develops in the team, you and your staff will make little progress. You'll have the opposite of what we want with an NDL. Everyone on your team will be running around seeing how long they

23 "Leading Through Gratitude: David Novak," Crazy Good Turns, podcast, https://podcasts.apple.com/au/podcast/leading-through-gratitude-david-novak/id1137217687?i=1000482923336.

can make their to-do list. When you reward, celebrate, and promote staff, be clear about how they focused and had direct impact on a few key things. When you send around promotion announcements, mention how the person said no to low-value things, which gave them time and energy to have a larger impact.

You don't have to wait for promotion time either. Proactively celebrate staff on your team for the things they did not waste time on. Celebrate staff who hit their goals, with fewer number of hours wasted. Celebrate staff who said no and stayed focused.

TELL YOUR TEAM WHAT YOU ARE NOT MEASURING

Most teams today operate with metrics galore, the more data we can use to assess performance the better. As we layer on more and more performance metrics, staff find it really hard to discern what is and is not important. Especially as the relative weighting seems to change every year. So tell staff what you are not using to measure performance. To you, as the leader, this might be obvious. Your answer might be "If management didn't say it was important then it's not." However, to staff it's never that clear. Staff may not trust what will be measured and try to run after everything instead of staying focused. You owe it to your team to tell them what's on the "we're not measuring" list. Tell them which performance indicators you won't use this year. It will focus the team on the metrics that are currently most relevant for the business. It will help the team run to the hard things you need to solve.

NOT DOING JOB DESCRIPTION

Why not bring the NDL concept into the way we design roles and hire? We can. In fact, I've seen it. An SVP, Operations role popped up on LinkedIn recently. It had seven succinct bullets describing the job. Then under the bullets it said in bold **WHAT YOU WON'T BE DOING**. It bluntly stated, "You won't have a sales goal, you won't do pseudo marketing work, you won't manage the data or systems." This is brilliant. Tell people what we don't want them to focus on before they even apply to our positions. It will attract people who understand their time, focus, and want to solve our hard problems. It will help attract people who want to spend their time on the core focus of the role.

MAKE SURE YOUR TEAM HAS FUN WITH THEIR NDL

When your team starts to casually joke about their NDL, you'll know you're in a great spot. If they comment to each other things like, "Put it on your NDL!" or "Sounds like an NDL meeting to me!" Then you know staff are thinking about it routinely. Encourage your team to use #NDL in messages back and forth to highlight things that are low-value and call out where they are not spending time. Think about the last time you got a good deal on something online. You saved money, right? Didn't you want to tell your friends or neighbors? Didn't a part of you want to say, "Look at me; I just saved $50!" Well, when you put something on your NDL, you're saving time. In essence, you're doing the same thing. You and your team should start to feel the same way about your #NDL. Staff will want to share this saved time with each other and maybe even brag about it. Celebrate what's on the list. Show off how much time you're saving. Let your team joke about it and poke some fun at the concept too. Having a laugh about what your team is choosing not to do is actually healthy.

CONCLUSION

I made you a promise when you started reading this book. I promised that, at a minimum, you would be able to find at least twenty hours of time to win back in the next three months. I promised a 100 percent return on the time you spent reading this book. Thinking back through all the rules, tactics, lessons, reminders, and examples, I'm confident we've exceeded this promise.

We've covered a lot, and we won't endeavor to recap it here. I'm sure I've missed things along the way. I'm sure I overlooked additional things you can save time not doing. I'm sure you'll discover your own tricks and techniques to make your list work. I'm sure there are extreme cases and circumstances that will require a more

MAKE NEXT WEEK THE WEEK YOU START SAYING NO.

advanced tool kit. My hope is that you view this book as basic when you look back months and years from now. That means you're pushing the envelope and winning back a ton of time. I also hope that soon you no longer need this book and all the steps of the NDL framework to win back time each week. Soon enough, it will be part of who you are and how you approach each and every day. Communicating that you're not doing something will seem simple and routine.

My parting advice is to start. Just start. Make next week the week you start saying no. Make it the week you start winning back your precious time. Make it the week you stay in send mode. Make it the week you skip at least one meeting, say no to one project, and avoid someone who might drop by and waste your time. Make it the week you finally shut your virtual door and respond only during predetermined hours. Make next week the week you skip that event. Make next week the week you choose to look past certain indicators or delete useless data. Make next week the week you timebox a project or set boundaries around when you won't worry. Make next week the week you'll stop covering for someone else. Make next week the week you delete more emails. Make next week the week you set a slower response time for certain people. Make next week the week you walk the other way to dodge an energy vampire.

What will you not do next week?

SHARE YOUR #NDL WITH OTHERS, GET
NEW IDEAS FOR WHAT NOT TO DO, AND
LEARN HOW OTHER LEADERS ARE SAYING
NO RIGHT NOW. JOIN THE CONVERSATION
AT WWW.NOTDOINGLIST.COM

EXERCISES TO HELP YOU JUMP- START YOUR NDL

The following is a set of exercises to help you build your first NDL. These short exercises coincide with the steps outlined previously. The prompts will help you generate ideas that can flow directly onto your NDL. Revisit the associated chapters for examples and tips. Remember that even filling in a few things from each step can yield a drastic amount of time savings across the coming weeks. Also, you don't have to make this formal. Make it your own and create a system of outlining what you won't do that works for you.

List your focus areas (remember, three at most). These can be near-term (thirty days out) or longer-term (a year or more). They can also change; this is just what you currently are trying to accomplish.

1. _____

2. _____

3. _____

Draft a one-sentence headline that describes what success at the end of next week sounds like:

(Remember this should tie to your focus areas.)

_____

_____

_____

STEP 1: QUIT WORTHLESS PROJECTS

Document three upcoming projects to consider for your NDL. These could be projects you know are coming up or ones you're currently working on.

1. _____

2. _____

STEP 2: HUNT FOR MEETINGS TO SKIP

Look back at your calendar for last week. Pinpoint three meetings that wasted your time, and complete the table here.

Meeting	Why the meeting wasted your time	Where else you could have invested that time
1.		
2.		
3.		

Hopefully that makes you a little angry. Now, take that anger and apply it forward. Look at your calendar for the next week, and find five meetings to consider skipping or canceling. Then add these to your NDL.

1. _____

2. _____

3. _____

4. _____

5. _____

STEP 3: CANCEL YOUR FLIGHTS

List your known work travel for the coming quarter and how it ties to achieving success in your focus areas. If you're struggling to see how it will support progress in these areas then strongly consider canceling the trip and adding it to your NDL.

Known or potential work trips	How many total hours will you spend planning and taking this trip?	How does this trip help you make true progress in your focus areas?	What better alternative way could you spend this time?	Is the time best spent on the trip or an alternative?
1.				Trip / Alternative
2.				Trip / Alternative
3.				Trip / Alternative
4.				Trip / Alternative
5.				Trip / Alternative

STEP 4: BLOCK THE REST OF YOUR CALENDAR

STEP 5: DODGE THE ENERGY VAMPIRES

Pinpoint the top three energy vampires in your organization. Then forecast when you will see them next and how they might strip you of your energy. Place these names on your NDL. You should also add the meeting, event, email, or other interaction where you think they might strike. We have to avoid the energy vampires at all costs.

Energy vampires (names)	When and how will this energy vampire potentially strike next
1.	
2.	
3	

STEP 6: REFUSE TO HELP ROLE JUSTIFIERS

Pinpoint the role justifiers and the make-work they might try to rope you into next week. Then add these names and their requests to your NDL.

Role justifiers (names)	What work will the role justifiers try to pull you into that is not important and does not tie to your headline?
1.	
2.	
3	

STEP 7: STOP DOING OTHERS' WORK

Pick out at least three things that you were planning to do next week that are actually part of someone else's role or responsibilities. List the task and who it should be reassigned to for ownership. Then ship it off and put it on your NDL.

Tasks to be sent back to proper owner	Who should the work be sent to?
1.	
2.	
3	

STEP 8: DECIDE WHO HAS TO ASK YOU TWICE

Who are three colleagues or three groups in your organization you likely respond to too quickly or provide more than you actually have to when they request your time or support? We learned that we should put in place Service Level Agreements (SLAs). Here we'll outline the appropriate SLA in terms of time and quality for when and how we'll respond to certain people. On the left, list who might require an SLA. Then list a more appropriate response time and what you should really be providing to them in terms of quality and quantity. Then write statements for your NDL on the right that describe what you won't do outside your SLA. Define how you will not respond too quickly or with more than is needed (e.g., Don't send data back to Jenni before 5:00 p.m.; do not build a new deck for Robert each week).

Who requires an SLA?	What is an appropriate SLA? (response time and quality/quantity of what you'll provide)	What will you not do for these colleagues? (put this on your NDL)
1.		
2.		
3.		

STEP 9: FIRE YOUR LEAST PROFITABLE CUSTOMERS

Which customers are least profitable for you this year? List customers that seem to require more time and energy than their revenue is worth. Take this list and discuss it with other colleagues to make sure you don't fire customers that will be key for your goals or the organization's overall revenue. Then add these customers to your NDL, and either minimize your service level or fire them completely.

Customer to fire #1: _____

Customer to fire #2: _____

Customer to fire #3: _____

STEP 10: PICK BATTLES TO LOSE

What new changes (policies, tools, procedures, etc.) do you know will be rolling out across your organization in the coming weeks or months? Decide if you can influence or change these and whether or not they directly influence your ability to achieve success in your focus areas. Pick those changes you will lose the battle against and put them on your NDL. The changes here could also be ongoing debates about a way forward within your team or business. You can use this exercise to pick those types of battles to lose too.

New change or on-going debate	Can you influence?	Does it directly impact your focus areas?	Can you just lose the battle and reinvest that time and energy?
1.	Yes/No	Yes/No	Yes/No
2.			
3.			

STEP 11: SCRUTINIZE SERVICE PROVIDERS TRYING TO "HELP"

List the service providers or their tools that could zap your time in the week ahead. Don't worry about the monetary costs; focus only on where your future time may be wasted with them, and write down their name. Also, jot down any notes about when you'll need to avoid them. Place the service provider and any meetings or emails on your NDL.

Services providers	When to avoid these providers (e.g., emails, meetings)
1.	
2.	
3	

STEP 12: SCALE BACK TIME
WITH UNDERPERFORMERS

Identify the low performers on your team and complete this simple worksheet to make sure you can confidently spend less time with them. If they meet the criteria, then place them on your NDL.

List under-performers (bottom 10 to 20 percent of your team in terms of performance)	Have you given them the support needed to improve performance? (if yes, consider for your NDL.)	Have you seen their performance improve at an acceptable rate? (If no, consider for your NDL.)	Have you clearly communicated they are not performing well and it might be time to look for a new role? (If yes, consider for your NDL.)
	Yes/No	Yes/No	Yes/No

Who are the new employees you should spend time with to help them get up to speed?

(*These employees should NOT go on your NDL.*)

1. _____

2. _____

3. _____

Who are the high-potential employees you should invest time in so they continue to grow their impact?

(These employees should NOT go on your NDL.)

1. _____

2. _____

3. _____

Who are the high-performing employees where you should spend time to help them run harder and faster against goals for your team?

(These employees should NOT go on your NDL.)

1. _____

2. _____

3. _____

STEP 13: DELETE DATA AND INFORMATION

Pick three sets of information and data that you don't need to be successful, and name them here. Select data that is irrelevant, inaccurate, or just "nice-to-have." These are the pieces of information that you can delete without needing to consume them each time you receive them. Add these to your NDL.

1. _____

2. _____

3. _____

STEP 14: CHOOSE BUSINESS PERFORMANCE INDICATORS TO IGNORE

Pick three performance indicators to ignore in the week ahead. These are indicators that don't relate to key business risks, are too narrow, don't have strong data accuracy, or are outdated. Add these to your NDL.

1. _____

2. _____

3. _____

STEP 15: SUSPEND USELESS REPORTS

Take a look at any reports or data that you're sending out to the rest of the organization. Assess who is actually consuming this information and what they are doing with it. List at least two things you are sending out each week that you can stop sending. Add these to your NDL.

1. _____

2. _____

STEP 16: ERASE YOUR "SOMEDAY" LIST

Find three things that have been on your to-do list forever that you will realistically never get to. Don't fear they will be gone forever. We're just writing them down for now. Put these items on your NDL.

1. _____

2. _____

3. _____

STEP 17: ELIMINATE, SHORTEN, OR AUTOMATE ROUTINE PROCESSES

List three processes or routine tasks that you could spend less time on if they were redesigned or automated. Then list which step you could eliminate or redesign to save you time. If you find quick things you can change next week, add them to your NDL. Many of these will likely be things that require planning and investment to change. Make sure to block time to work on these so you can continue to win back more time in future weeks.

Process or recurring task	What can I eliminate, redesign, or automate and still get the same result?
1.	
2.	
3	

STEP 18: TIMEBOX LIMITLESS TASKS

Look out across the coming week, and ask yourself, *What are the tasks that could take an unlimited amount of time if not controlled?* These are the tasks that might need to be timeboxed. Write the task and then the amount of time you will give yourself to work on the task. You're estimating the point of diminishing marginal return (when you'll get to good enough for this task) and setting a limit for yourself. Write these as statements on your NDL in a way that holds you accountable for spending only a certain amount of time (e.g., Don't spend more than ___ hours on task ___).

Upcoming task that should be timeboxed	How much time will you give yourself for this task?
1.	
2.	
3	

STEP 19: GO HEAVY ON THE DELETE KEY

What percentage of your (nonspam) email will you delete without a response this week? _____ percent

How long will you spend on email each day this week to clear out your inbox? _____ minutes per day

What times during each day will you check and respond to email?

Monday: _____

Tuesday: _____

Wednesday: _____

Thursday: _____

Friday: _____

STEP 20: PICK PROBLEMS YOU WON'T SOLVE

Keep a list of the problems you know that your team or organization has. Then score the relative impact of solving these challenges in terms of the impact it will have on your team or organization. Then score the level of effort required to solve these challenges for your team or organization. Use the relative weightings to find the problems that are high effort and low impact, and put those on your NDL. Remember that we're not agreeing to never solve this problem, just not right now.

Problems identified on your team or in the organization	How will solving this problem impact your team or organization's ability to achieve your goals? (Scale from 1 to 10) 1 = no impact, 10 = significant impact	How hard will it be to solve this problem for your team or organization? (Scale from 1 to 10) 1 = easy, 10 = hard	Should this be a problem I ignore for now and place on my NDL?
1.			
2.			
3.			

STEP 21: FIND PERSONAL PERFORMANCE GAPS TO NOT CLOSE

Take your known development opportunities or performance gaps, and bucket them into these three categories. Remember, you should work with your boss to get feedback and make sure they agree with your distribution.

What gaps are not allowing you to be most effective in your current role?

1. _____

2. _____

3. _____

Which gaps are holding you back from the next role?

1. _____

2. _____

3. _____

Which gaps are more opportunistic in nature that your boss believes may hinder you long term?

1. _____

2. _____

3. _____

Knowing you can't close all gaps at once, decide which are least important for where you're going next. Select at least one and place it on your NDL.

STEP 22 TO 27: DESIGN A DISTRACTION-LESS DAY

Pinpoint four distractions that could steal your attention next week and when they might pop up. Write down the distraction, when the distraction might strike, and your approach to tune it out. Place these on your NDL (e.g., "Avoid Twitter between 2:00 and 5:00 p.m. by turning my phone off").

As a reminder here are the common distractions previously covered that you should consider dodging by putting freezes on your NDL.

Step 22: Freeze Instant Messaging

Step 23: Freeze Social Media

Step 24: Freeze News and Media

Step 25: Freeze Your Email

Step 26: Turn Your Phone Off

Step 27: Declare No Multitasking Time

Distractions	When might this distraction strike? (specific days and times)	How can I freeze this distraction? (e.g., turn off phone)
1.		
2.		
3.		
4.		

STEP 28: ELIMINATE UNPRODUCTIVE WORRYING

Pinpoint three things you could worry about that will cause anxiety next week and when they might cross your mind. Also, select a worry slot, which is a specific time set aside to worry about the thing in question later in the week. Add these things to your NDL. Book a worry slot on your calendar to do the worrying.

Things that might pop up and cause anxiety this week	When might this cross your mind?	When is your dedicated worry slot? (e.g., Friday at 1 p.m.)
1.		
2.		
3.		

NOT DOING LIST

CPSIA information can be obtained
at www.ICGtesting.com
Printed in the USA
JSHW020824310321
13073JS00008B/115